The
Superfood
KITCHEN

The Superfood KITCHEN

This edition published by Parragon Books Ltd in 2015
LOVE FOOD is an imprint of Parragon Books Ltd

Parragon Books Ltd
Chartist House
15–17 Trim Street
Bath BA1 1HA, UK
www.parragon.com/lovefood

ISBN: 978-1-4723-6454-8

Printed in China

New recipes and food styling by Sara Lewis
Created and produced by Pene Parker and Becca Spry
New photography by Haarala Hamilton

Notes for the reader

This book uses both metric and imperial measurements. Follow the same units of measurement
throughout; do not mix metric and imperial. All spoon measurements are level: teaspoons are
assumed to be 5 ml and tablespoons are assumed to be 15 ml. Unless otherwise stated, milk is
assumed to be full fat, eggs and individual vegetables are medium, and pepper is freshly ground
black pepper. Unless otherwise stated, all root vegetables should be peeled prior to use.

Garnishes, decorations and serving suggestions are all optional and not necessarily included
in the recipe ingredients or method. Any optional ingredients and seasoning to taste are not
included in the nutritional analysis. The times given are an approximate guide only. Preparation
times differ according to the techniques used by different people and the cooking times may also
vary from those given. Optional ingredients, variations or serving suggestions have not been
included in the time calculations.

While the author has made all reasonable efforts to ensure that the information contained in
this book is accurate and up to date at the time of publication, anyone reading this book should
note the following important points:
* Medical and pharmaceutical knowledge is constantly changing and the author and the publisher
cannot and do not guarantee the accuracy or appropriateness of the contents of this book;
* In any event, this book is not intended to be, and should not be relied upon as, a substitute for
appropriate, tailored professional advice. Both the author and the publisher strongly
recommend that a doctor or other healthcare professional is consulted before embarking on
major dietary changes;
* For the reasons set out above, and to the fullest extent permitted by law, the author and
publisher: (i) cannot and do not accept any legal duty of care or responsibility in relation to the
accuracy or appropriateness of the contents of this book, even where expressed as 'advice' or
using other words to this effect; and (ii) disclaim any liability, loss, damage or risk that may be
claimed or incurred as a consequence – directly or indirectly – of the use and/or application of
any of the contents of this book.

CONTENTS

WHAT IS A SUPERFOOD?

'Superfoods' have been celebrated by nutritionists as being beneficial for health and well-being for years. These nutrient-dense ingredients offer a bundle of essential vitamins, minerals, protein, complex carbohydrates and good monounsaturated and polyunsaturated fats. A balanced intake of these nutrients is crucial for energy, growth, repair, immunity and essential metabolic processes. The good news doesn't stop there though – superfoods are also rich in antioxidants and phytochemicals, which can help protect us against cancers, coronary heart disease, strokes, diabetes and obesity. No wonder we so often hear that superfoods should be top of our shopping list!

Superfoods can be bought easily from supermarkets, farmers' markets and health-food shops and are often inexpensive. Thanks to their health-boosting qualities, they could almost be called 'natural medicines', but no prescription is required and there are no negative side-effects so long as they are eaten as part of a balanced diet.

The brighter the colour of a fruit or vegetable, the more beneficial to health it is likely to be. Choose from deep-purple blueberries, ruby-red strawberries and raspberries, bright-orange pumpkins, carrots and mangoes and deep-green broccoli and kale. Plant foods are packed with antioxidants and phytochemicals (biologically active plant chemicals). These help to reduce the activity of free radicals – harmful compounds produced by the body, which damage DNA and body tissues – and so they are believed to help protect the body against cancer.

Wash or scrub fruits and vegetables and eat them with the skins on where possible to boost their fibre, vitamin and mineral levels. There's no need to peel apples, pears, peaches or young carrots. This is an easy way to add natural soluble fibre to your diet, which will help stave off mid-morning or mid-afternoon munchies, and to lower cholesterol and protect against bowel cancer.

Plants aren't the only superfoods. Nuts, seeds, wholegrains, oily fish and natural live yogurt are other examples of nutrient-dense, power-packed ingredients.

When altering your diet, take small steps that you can build on rather than making major dietary changes that you will struggle to maintain. There's a lot of truth in the expression 'we are what we eat', and eating a range of superfoods should help you to feel fitter, lighter and more energized, and to cope with the hustle and bustle of modern living, while improving your long-term health.

WHAT IS A HEALTHY DIET?

The key to a healthy diet is variety, so try to eat a mix of many types of foods. Dishes offering low nutritional value, such as sugar- and fat-laden cakes and biscuits, can harm you if eaten in large quantities or over a long period of time, as they have been linked to obesity, diabetes, high cholesterol and heart problems, and even cancer. There is nothing wrong with the odd treat, but keep a burger and chips or a gooey slice of chocolate cake as just that, an occasional treat.

In Western countries, 21st-century diseases are more commonly caused by dietary excess and imbalance than by nutritional deficiency. It is important to eat foods from all the main food groups: carbohydrates, proteins, fats, vitamins and minerals. But some foods are better than others. Opt for wholegrain carbohydrates, rich in fibre, as these take a long time to digest, leaving you feeling fuller for longer and releasing energy slowly to help you avoid mood swings and lethargy, and are thought to help lower cholesterol.

Add sugar to foods sparingly, if at all, choosing naturally sweet fruits and dried fruits in place of highly refined white sugar.

Rather than butter and cream, choose virgin cold-pressed oils such as olive or rapeseed oil, or try hemp, flaxseed or walnut oils. Low-fat live yogurt, cottage cheese or cream cheese, or ricotta, also make healthy options. Grill meat and fish rather than frying them to lower your fat intake, and choose 'clean' meats such as protein-rich skinless turkey breast, which is low in saturated fat – the primary cause of clogged arteries. When using hard cheeses such as Cheddar, Gruyère or Parmesan, which are high in fat, grate them so that a little goes a long way.

Cut back on salt. Junk food and chilled ready-meals and snacks all tend to be high in hidden salt. By reducing your intake of these, or cutting them out, you will lower your salt intake.

Remember, food doesn't always need to be cooked – increase your intake of crisp leafy salads, fruity salsas and fruit salads. Rather than snacking on crisps or biscuits, have an apple or a handful of dried goji berries or dates.

20 FABULOUS SUPERFOODS

1 Go for green – the deeper green veg are, the more lutein and zeaxanthin (two antioxidants related to vitamin A) they are likely to contain. Broccoli, cabbage, chard, kale, rocket, spinach and watercress are rich in chlorophyll, which assists with the oxygenation and health of blood cells, so helping to fight fatigue. They are also good sources of the B vitamins, especially folic acid, as well as immune-boosting vitamin C, and vitamin K for strong bones and healthy blood clotting. Kale is a useful source of iron. Broccoli and cauliflower belong to the cruciferous family and are good sources of sulphurous compounds, which may help protect against cancer.

2 Red fruit bonanza – summery red berries such as strawberries and raspberries are rich in vitamin C, which aids healing and fights infection, and fibre. Cranberries help block bacterial growth, especially in the urinary tract. Their relative, the blueberry, is very high in antioxidants, pectin to help lower cholesterol, and vitamin C. Pomegranates also contain antioxidant vitamins, as well as iron and fibre. Although high in water, red-fleshed watermelons contain antioxidants, folic acid, potassium, and vitamins A and C. Pink and ruby grapefruits, along with other members of the citrus family and kiwi fruits, are bursting with vitamin C, as well as minerals and antioxidants. Power-packed with antioxidants, iron, fibre and vitamin C, dried goji berries make a great storecupboard standby. Tomatoes get their red colour from lycopene, a carotenoid pigment which, along with the other antioxidants tomatoes contain, may help protect against free-radical damage and prostate cancer and prevent blood clots.

3 Red veg bonanza – red beetroot gets its red pigment from the antioxidants betalains, which help protect against free-radical damage and may help reduce the risk of heart disease, and it provides a wide range of vitamins, minerals and carbohydrates. All peppers contain vitamin C, but red peppers contain the most, followed by orange and yellow, then green. They are rich in antioxidants and bioflavonoids, which help neutralize free-radical damage and so are thought to help protect against cancer.

4 Sunshine fruits and vegetables – rich in beta-carotene, this bright-orange group contains carrots, pumpkins, butternut squash, sweet potatoes, papayas, mangoes and apricots. Beta-carotene is needed by the body to make vitamin A, an antioxidant thought to help protect against cancer, and is important for the integrity of each cell and to boost the immune system.

5 Autumn's apples and pears – apples are rich in pectin (the setting agent in jam), which helps to remove excess cholesterol and toxic metals from the digestive tract while stimulating the growth of friendly bacteria in the large intestine, boosting vitamin C and providing a naturally sweet energy lift. Pears are healthy too, and packed with fibre.

6 Eggs and low-fat and probiotic yogurts – eggs are power-packed with protein. Low-fat yogurts make a good replacement for cream as a dessert topping or base for frozen desserts, salad dressings and marinades, and the calcium and phosphorus they contain helps boost bone strength. Probiotic yogurts are thought to help maintain and promote healthy bacterial balance in the intestine and bowel, and strengthen your natural defences, which is especially useful after a course of antibiotics, as these can kill good bacteria as well as bad.

7 Fab fish – salmon, trout, herring, mackerel, fresh tuna and sardines are oily fish, and are rich in protein, needed for growth and the maintenance of cells. They're packed with Omega-3 essential fatty acids, which help protect against heart and circulation problems and aid healthy development of the eyes and brain of a baby during pregnancy. They're a good source of minerals: selenium for growth and fertility, iodine for healthy function of the thyroid gland, vitamin B12 for the nervous system, and vitamin D for healthy bones and teeth. Try to eat one portion each week.

8 Sustaining wholegrains – avoid highly refined rice and flours. Choose brown rice for higher vitamin B levels and fibre. Opt for brown wholewheat or wholemeat flour for maximum fibre, or try wheat-free, gluten-free flours, such as buckwheat flour, brown rice flour or hemp flour. Porridge oats and oatmeal make a sustaining, warming breakfast or muesli base, and taste great in cakes and bakes. Cook oat or barley groats or wheatberries in boiling water as an alternative to rice. Look out for wholegrain couscous and quinoa, the only grain to contain all the essential amino acids the body requires. Rich in fibre, wholegrains leave you feeling fuller for longer and help maintain a healthy digestive system, lower cholesterol and aid good heart health.

9 Power pulses – choose pulses either dried or canned in water for a cheap, low-fat base to any meal. They taste great mixed with vegetables and spices, and a little added to meat or poultry makes a meal go further. Dried pulses include dried cannellini beans, flageolet beans and red kidney beans, to name just a few. They all require soaking in cold water overnight and then boiling in water before use. Red lentils, which make a good base for dal; puy or brown lentils, which are great as a salad base; or the larger green lentils, can all be used without soaking and are a good source of protein, B vitamins and minerals. The fibre they contain helps to lower blood cholesterol, while the starch is digested and absorbed by the body slowly to give a sustained energy release.

10 Nuts and seeds – packed with protein, nuts supply many of the same minerals that meat does, such as B vitamins, phosphorus, iron, copper and potassium, so are good for vegetarians. They are high in fat, so add them to dishes in small amounts. Nuts are one of the richest sources of vitamin E, but this is destroyed when they are roasted, so eat raw when you can. Supermarkets now sell hemp, flaxseeds and chia seeds as well as pumpkin, sunflower and sesame seeds. Ideally grind or chop them, so the body is able to absorb as many of the nutrients as possible. Finely ground seeds can be used in much the same way as ground almonds. Like nuts, seeds are high in calories. Flaxseeds are rich in B vitamins, magnesium and manganese, plus Omega-3 and -6 essential fatty acids. Chia seeds are also a good source of essential fatty acids as well as calcium, iron, copper and zinc. Hemp seeds are the only seeds to contain all the essential amino acids.

11 Dates – a natural source of sweetness, dates contain fibre, potassium, manganese, magnesium and vitamins A, B6 and K. Due to the fibre content, they're thought to help maintain a healthy colon.

12 Secrets of soya – the Chinese and Japanese have long enjoyed soya beans and tofu. Soya is rich in protein and contains all the essential amino acids, vitamin E and B vitamins, calcium, iron and antioxidants, while being low in fat. Fibre-rich baby green soya beans are sold frozen. Soya milk, made from the soaked ground beans, can be used instead of dairy milk in most recipes. Tofu is made from soya beans; dice it and add it to vegetable stews, noodle dishes or soups, or marinade in soy sauce, ginger and garlic, then grill, dice and add to salads or stir-fries. Soya helps to protect against heart disease, osteoporosis and menopausal symptoms.

13 Amazing alliums – garlic has been used for centuries to help fight infections, as it acts as an anti-microbial agent. Leeks are another allium with superfood properties, and are particularly notable for their concentration of the B vitamin folate, while their antioxidant and flavonoid properties mean they help protect our blood vessels and blood cells.

14 Jerusalem artichokes – packed with inulin, these knobbly roots are thought to aid beneficial bacteria in the gut, while their high fibre and water content help keep our bowels healthy. They are also a good source of potassium.

15 Energizing bananas – a banana is a terrific high-energy snack, and a great source of natural fruit sugars, starch and potassium to help regulate blood pressure and lower the risk of heart attacks and strokes. It is the only fruit to contain both the amino acid tryptophan and vitamin B6, which together produce the natural chemical serotonin, making it a good-mood-food.

16 Amazing avocados – the avocado contains even more potassium than the banana. Thought to be one of the most nutritionally complete fruits, it is rich in vitamins, minerals, phytonutrients, the antioxidant lutein and protein.

17 Sprouting seeds – think of sprouting seeds, sometimes called salad sprouts, as a nutritional powerhouse. As the seeds germinate and begin to sprout, their natural nutrients multiply to meet the growing needs of the young shoots. This makes them a good way to add a range of antioxidants and immune-boosting vitamins, minerals and protein to a dish. As the seeds sprout, so the plant enzymes increase, and this aids digestion. Children younger than five, older adults, pregnant women and those with a weakened immune system are particularly vulnerable to the bacteria that may be present on sprouts and so should not eat raw sprouts. Buy pre-packed sprouts from the shops or grow them from a kit following the manufacturer's instructions and wash them well.

18 Turkey – high in concentrated protein, skinless and boneless turkey is very low in fat, saturated fat and sodium.

19 Plain chocolate – choose chocolate that has over 65 per cent cocoa. The higher the cocoa content, the higher the flavonoids, which help to reduce infection and protect cells from damage. Plain chocolate also contains the mineral magnesium, which is needed for nerve and muscle function, and the amino acid tryptophan, which is used by the body to make serotonin.

20 Green tea – long favoured by the Chinese, green tea contains an enhanced level of antioxidants. It is thought to have antibacterial and antiviral properties. Many people believe it can help boost metabolism, aid blood pressure and reduce bad cholesterol.

SUPER INGREDIENTS

Maca – a small, round root that was first grown in the Andes. It is thought to help fight fatigue and menopausal and menstrual discomfort and depression. It is available from health-food shops in powder form, and can be mixed into porridge, smoothies or nut milks. It's a rich source of protein, minerals and C, E and B-group vitamins.

Spirulina – a dark green algae, usually sold in powder form, which is rich in chlorophyll, calcium, protein, essential fatty acids and vitamin B12. Stir it into juices and smoothies.

Wheatgrass – you can buy wheatgrass as fresh grass in trays from health-food shops. Press it through a juicer, then mix it with banana or another sweet-tasting fruit, as it has a strong taste. Powdered wheatgrass is much easier to use; simply stir a teaspoon or two into smoothies, juices or salad dressings, but be aware that it will turn everything very dark green. It contains chlorophyll, A, C, K and B-group vitamins, iron and potassium.

SUPERFOODS DAY BY DAY

The more superfoods you eat, the less room you will have for unhealthy foods. It doesn't take long to make a healthy stir-fry or salad. For lunch, top up sandwiches with grated carrot or salad leaves, or pack a small pot of three-bean salad or coleslaw made with French dressing rather than mayonnaise, plus fresh or dried fruits.

Most fruits and vegetables are low-calorie, so portion sizes can be generous. Keep a bag of apples in your desk rather than biscuits or chocolate. Nuts and seeds are easy to nibble on, and are packed with protein and healthy fats – but try not to eat too many as they are high in calories.

Changing your diet needn't increase your food bill. For example, homemade soup can be quick and inexpensive to make, and extra portions can be frozen for an easy lunch. Frozen fruit, peas, green beans, sweetcorn and fish make handy standbys and can contain more vitamins and minerals than fresh ones that have sat in the refrigerator for too long.

Plan your weekly suppers; it makes shopping easier and quicker and there will be less temptation to buy junk food and processed chilled meals.

BREAKFASTS

Red beetroot hash	20
Eggs in pepper and tomato sauce	22
Cinnamon pancakes with tropical fruit salad	24
Jumbo carrot cake biscuits	26
Banana, goji and hazelnut bread	28
Barley porridge with grilled papaya and peaches	30
Apple and seed muesli	33
Fruity granola cups	34
Strawberry breakfast dip	37
Yogurt with blueberries, honey and nuts	38
Mango and kale juice	40
Avocado and fruit juice	42

RED BEETROOT HASH

A vegetable hash is the perfect Saturday brunch. This dish contains antioxidant-rich sweet potatoes, low-carbohydrate Jerusalem artichokes and cholesterol-lowering beetroot.

SERVES: 4   PREP: 20 MINS   COOK: 40 MINS

350 g/12 oz Jerusalem artichokes, unpeeled and scrubbed
450 g/1 lb raw beetroot, cut into cubes
750 g/1 lb 10 oz sweet potatoes, cut into cubes
2 tbsp olive oil
1 red onion, roughly chopped
2 tsp mild paprika
1/2 tsp mustard powder
3 tsp fresh thyme leaves, plus extra to garnish
4 eggs
salt and pepper

1 Halve any of the larger artichokes. Half-fill the base of a steamer with water, bring to the boil, then add the artichokes to the water. Put the beetroot in one half of the steamer top, cover with a lid and steam for 10 minutes. Put the sweet potatoes in the other half of the top, so the colour of the beetroot won't bleed into the sweet potatoes. Cover with a lid again and steam for 10 minutes more, or until all the vegetables are just tender. Drain the artichokes, peel them and cut them into cubes.

2 Heat 1 tablespoon of oil in a large frying pan over a medium heat. Add the red onion and fry for 3–4 minutes, or until beginning to soften. Add the artichokes, beetroot and sweet potatoes and fry for 10 minutes, or until browned.

3 Stir in the paprika, mustard powder and thyme and season well with salt and pepper. Make four spaces in the frying pan, drizzle in the remaining oil, then crack an egg into each hole. Sprinkle the eggs with salt and pepper, then cover and cook for 4–5 minutes, or until the eggs are cooked to your liking. Spoon onto plates and serve immediately, garnished with extra thyme.

DETOX WITH ARTICHOKES

Knobbly-looking Jerusalem artichokes contain several phytonutrients, which are thought to help detoxify the liver and boost gall bladder function. They are also considered to help digestion. What's more, they're packed with fibre, helping you to feel fuller for longer.

PER SERVING: 430 CALS | 12.6G FAT | 2.7G SAT FAT | 67.4G CARBS | 25.3G SUGARS | 1.4G SALT | 11.1G FIBRE | 14G PROTEIN

EGGS IN PEPPER AND TOMATO SAUCE

Protein-packed eggs are star of the show in this simple one-pan brunch that's bursting with superfoods.

SERVES: 4   PREP: 20 MINS   COOK: 30 MINS

4 large tomatoes
1½ tbsp rapeseed oil
1 large onion, finely chopped
½ tsp coriander seeds, crushed
½ tsp caraway seeds, crushed
2 red peppers, deseeded and roughly chopped
¼ tsp dried red chilli flakes
1 large garlic clove, thinly sliced
4 eggs
salt and pepper
1 tbsp roughly chopped fresh flat-leaf parsley, to garnish

1 Put the tomatoes in a shallow bowl and cover with boiling water. Leave for 30 seconds, then drain. Slip off the skins and discard, then chop the tomatoes.

2 Heat the oil in a large frying pan over a medium heat. Add the onion, coriander seeds and caraway seeds. Fry, stirring occasionally, for 10 minutes, or until the onion is soft and golden.

3 Stir in the red peppers and chilli flakes and fry for 5 minutes more, or until softened.

4 Add the garlic and tomatoes with their seeds and juices and season with salt and pepper. Reduce the heat to low and simmer, uncovered, for 10 minutes.

5 Crack the eggs over the surface. Cover and cook for a further 4–5 minutes, or until the eggs are cooked to your liking. Season with salt and pepper, sprinkle with the parsley and serve immediately.

TASTY TOMATOES

Tomatoes contain vitamins A, C and E, as well as zinc and selenium, all of which can help disarm free radicals that are produced when the body is under stress.

PER SERVING: 181 CALS | 11G FAT | 2.2G SAT FAT | 12G CARBS | 6.9G SUGARS | 0.9G SALT | 3.2G FIBRE | 9G PROTEIN

CINNAMON PANCAKES WITH TROPICAL FRUIT SALAD

Everyone loves pancakes, big or small, and these French-style crêpes are sure to be a hit. Make the fruit salad the night before and keep it in the refrigerator to save time.

SERVES: 4   PREP: 25 MINS   COOK: 25 MINS

100 g/3$\frac{1}{2}$ oz wholemeal plain flour
$\frac{1}{2}$ tsp ground cinnamon
2 eggs, beaten
225 ml/8 fl oz unsweetened soya milk
3 tbsp water
3 tbsp sunflower oil

FRUIT SALAD
1 ruby grapefruit
250 g/9 oz pineapple flesh, cut into cubes
150 g/5$\frac{1}{2}$ oz mango flesh, cut into cubes
finely grated zest of $\frac{1}{2}$ lime

TO SERVE
300 g/10$\frac{1}{2}$ oz natural soya yogurt
2 tbsp date syrup
40 g/1$\frac{1}{2}$ oz Brazil nuts, roughly chopped (optional)

1 For the fruit salad, cut the peel and pith away from the grapefruit with a small serrated knife. Hold it above a bowl and cut between the membranes to release the segments into the bowl. Squeeze the juice from the membranes into the bowl. Add the pineapple, mango and lime zest and mix well.

2 For the pancakes, put the flour and cinnamon in another bowl. Add the eggs, then gradually whisk in the soya milk until smooth. Whisk in the water and 1 tablespoon of oil.

3 Heat a little oil in an 18-cm/7-inch frying pan over a medium heat, then pour out the excess oil. Pour in one-eighth of the batter, tilting the pan to swirl the batter into an even layer. Cook for 2 minutes, or until the underside is golden.

4 Loosen the pancake, then flip it over with a palette knife and cook the second side for 1 minute, or until golden. Slide out of the pan and keep hot on a plate while you make seven more thin pancakes in the same way.

5 Arrange two folded pancakes on each of four plates and top with the fruit salad. Serve with a spoonful of the yogurt, drizzled with the date syrup. Top with the nuts, if using.

EGGSTRA SPECIAL

Just one medium egg contains 6.8 g protein. They are also loaded with selenium, iron, B vitamins and folic acid. They contain the antioxidant lutein too, which is believed to help protect against cataracts.

PER SERVING: 375 CALS | 14.2G FAT | 2.8G SAT FAT | 53.6G CARBS | 27.4G SUGARS | 0.2G SALT | 6.1G FIBRE | 13.7G PROTEIN

JUMBO CARROT CAKE BISCUITS

These dairy-free biscuits are made with coconut oil and sweetened with maple syrup, dried apricots, apple and carrot. They're great for breakfast on the go.

MAKES: 12 BISCUITS   PREP: 30 MINS   COOK: 20 MINS

100 g/3½ oz flaxseeds
85 g/3 oz wholemeal plain flour
70 g/2½ oz porridge oats
1 tsp baking powder
1 tsp ground ginger
2 tsp ground cinnamon
85 g/3 oz dried apricots, finely chopped
1 dessert apple, cored and coarsely grated
1 carrot, finely grated
40 g/1½ oz pecan nuts, roughly chopped
3 tbsp coconut oil
125 ml/4 fl oz maple syrup
grated zest of ½ orange, plus 3 tbsp juice
4 tbsp dried coconut shavings

1 Preheat the oven to 180°C/350°F/Gas Mark 4 and line two baking sheets with baking paper.

2 Put the flaxseeds in a blender and process to a fine powder, then tip into a mixing bowl. Add the flour, oats and baking powder, then the ginger and cinnamon, and stir well. Add the dried apricots, apple, carrot and pecan nuts and stir again.

3 Warm the coconut oil in a small saucepan (or in the microwave for 30 seconds) until just liquid. Remove from the heat, then stir in the maple syrup and orange zest and juice. Pour this into the carrot mixture and stir until you have a soft dough.

4 Spoon 12 mounds of the mixture onto the prepared baking sheets, then flatten them into thick 7.5-cm/3-inch diameter rounds. Sprinkle with the coconut shavings, then bake for 15–18 minutes, or until browned.

5 Serve warm or leave to cool, then pack into a plastic container and store in the fridge for up to three days.

CARROTS FOR YOUR EYES

The carotenoid pigment, beta-carotene, that gives carrots, butternut squash and sweet potatoes their bright-orange colour, is converted by the body into vitamin A, which is considered to be good for helping you to see in poor light.

PER BISCUIT: 208 CALS | 10.5G FAT | 4G SAT FAT | 27G CARBS | 12.6G SUGARS | 0.3G SALT | 5.5G FIBRE | 4.2G PROTEIN

BANANA, GOJI AND HAZELNUT BREAD

On mornings when you don't have time to eat breakfast before you leave for work, wrap a slice or two of this superfood-packed bread in baking paper and eat when you get there.

MAKES: 10 SLICES
PREP: 20 MINS, PLUS COOLING   COOK: 1 HOUR

85 g/3 oz butter, softened, plus extra to grease
115 g/4 oz light muscovado sugar
2 eggs
3 bananas (500 g/1 lb 2 oz with the skins on), peeled and mashed
115 g/4 oz wholemeal plain flour
115 g/4 oz plain flour
2 tsp baking powder
55 g/2 oz unblanched hazelnuts, roughly chopped
40 g/1½ oz goji berries
40 g/1½ oz dried banana chips

1 Preheat the oven to 180°C/350°F/Gas Mark 4. Grease a 900-g/2-lb loaf tin and line the base and two long sides with a piece of baking paper.

2 Cream the butter and sugar together in a large bowl. Beat in the eggs, one at a time, then the bananas.

3 Put the flours and baking powder in a bowl and mix well. Add to the banana mixture and beat until smooth. Add the hazelnuts and goji berries and stir well.

4 Spoon the mixture into the prepared tin, smooth the top flat then sprinkle with the banana chips. Bake for 50–60 minutes, or until the loaf is well risen, has cracked slightly and a skewer comes out cleanly when inserted into the centre.

5 Leave to cool for 5 minutes, then loosen the edges with a round-bladed knife and turn out onto a wire rack. Leave to cool completely, then peel away the paper. Store in an airtight tin for up to three days.

HIGH-ENERGY BANANAS

Naturally rich in fruit sugar and starch, bananas are a great energy-boosting food. They contain lots of potassium, which can help to regulate blood pressure and lower the risk of heart attacks and strokes. They also contain the amino acid tryptophan and vitamin B6, which together help in the production of mood-boosting serotonin.

PER SLICE: 276 CALS | 10G FAT | 2.5G SAT FAT | 43G CARBS | 19G SUGARS | 0.8G SALT | 3.5G FIBRE | 5.5G PROTEIN

BARLEY PORRIDGE WITH GRILLED PAPAYA AND PEACHES

Forget about thick, stodgy porridge, this healthier, lighter, dairy-free version is made with high-fibre barley flakes for an energizing start to the day.

SERVES: 4   PREP: 10 MINS   COOK: 10 MINS

85 g/3 oz barley flakes
85 g/3 oz porridge oats
350 ml/12 fl oz cold water
750 ml/1¼ pints unsweetened almond milk
4 tsp maca (see page 16)
2 peaches, halved, stoned and sliced
1 papaya, halved, deseeded, peeled and sliced
4 tsp runny honey, plus extra to serve
½ tsp ground cinnamon

1 Put the barley flakes, porridge oats, water and almond milk in a saucepan. Bring to the boil over a medium-high heat, then reduce the heat to medium and simmer for 5–10 minutes, stirring often, until soft and thickened. Stir in the maca.

2 Meanwhile, preheat the grill to medium–high. Line the grill rack with foil, then lay the peaches and papaya on top, drizzle with the honey and sprinkle with the cinnamon. Grill for 3–4 minutes, or until hot and just beginning to caramelize.

3 Spoon the porridge into bowls, top with the hot peaches and papaya and drizzle with a little extra honey, if liked.

POWER PAPAYA

The beautiful, orangey-yellow tropical papaya is bursting with vitamin C, potassium and folic acid. It also contains vitamins A and E, two antioxidants that are thought to protect against heart disease and colon cancer. Papayas are believed to be good for the skin, protecting against wrinkles, and for the eyes.

PER SERVING: 291 CALS | 4.3G FAT | 0.5G SAT FAT | 58G CARBS | 25.3G SUGARS | 0.2G SALT | 8.5G FIBRE | 8.3G PROTEIN

APPLE AND SEED
MUESLI

Nutty and fruity, this is a delicious and healthy start to the day.
Serve it with milk or live yogurt.

SERVES: 10
PREP: 15 MINS, PLUS COOLING   COOK: 4 MINS

75 g/2³/4 oz sunflower seeds
50 g/1³/4 oz pumpkin seeds
90 g/3¹/4 oz hazelnuts, roughly chopped
125 g/4¹/2 oz buckwheat flakes
125 g/4¹/2 oz rice flakes
125 g/4¹/2 oz millet flakes
115 g/4 oz no-soak dried apple, roughly chopped
115 g/4 oz stoned dried dates, roughly chopped

1 Place a frying pan over a medium heat. Add the sunflower seeds, pumpkin seeds and hazelnuts and toast, shaking the pan frequently, for 4 minutes, or until golden brown. Transfer to a large bowl and leave to cool.

2 Add the buckwheat flakes, rice flakes, millet flakes, dried apple and dates to the bowl and mix well. Store in an airtight container for up to five days.

BRILLIANT BUCKWHEAT

Buckwheat is a seed, although many people mistakenly think of it as a grain. It is a nutrition power-house, containing lots of protein. Because of its amino acid content it can boost the protein content of beans and grains eaten on the same day. It is also a good source of fibre.

PER SERVING: 319 CALS | 13G FAT | 1.4G SAT FAT | 47.9G CARBS | 15.5G SUGARS | TRACE SALT | 5.6G FIBRE | 8.9G PROTEIN

FRUITY GRANOLA CUPS

Granola is easy to make, and a brilliant stand-by ingredient –
just add yogurt and fruit when you're ready for your breakfast!

SERVES: 6   PREP: 25 MINS   COOK: 35 MINS

115 g/4 oz medium oatmeal
85 g/3 oz porridge oats
40 g/1½ oz unblanched almonds, roughly chopped
2 tbsp pumpkin seeds
2 tbsp sunflower seeds
2 tbsp flaxseeds, coarsely ground
½ tsp ground cinnamon
3 tbsp maple syrup
1 tbsp olive oil
25 g/1 oz goji berries

TO SERVE (SERVES 2)

115 g/4 oz granola
juice of 1 orange
115 g/4 oz Greek-style natural yogurt
1 dessert apple, cored and coarsely grated
115 g/4 oz strawberries, hulled and sliced
40 g/1½ oz blueberries

1 Preheat the oven to 160°C/325°F/Gas Mark 3. Put the oatmeal, porridge oats and almonds in a bowl. Stir in the pumpkin seeds, sunflower seeds and flaxseeds, then the cinnamon, maple syrup and oil.

2 Tip the granola into a roasting tin, then spread into an even layer. Bake for 30–35 minutes, or until golden brown all over, stirring every 5–10 minutes and mixing any browner granola from the edges of the tin into the centre after 15 minutes.

3 Stir in the goji berries, then leave to cool. Pack into an airtight container and store in the refrigerator for up to five days.

4 When ready to serve, spoon the granola into two glasses or bowls, keeping a little back for the top. Moisten with the orange juice. Mix the yogurt with the apple, spoon over the granola, top with the strawberries and blueberries and sprinkle with the remaining granola.

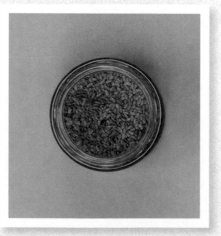

PROTECTIVE FLAXSEEDS

Grinding flaxseeds in a blender or spice mill means you can use them in cooking in the same way as ground almonds. It also means they are in a form that the body can process more easily, so that larger amounts of the essential Omega-3 fatty acids, needed for heart health, can be absorbed. They are rich in lignans, antioxidants that help protect the body against cancer, and in B vitamins, minerals and fibre.

PER SERVING: 402 CALS | 13.4G FAT | 1.6G SAT FAT | 57.6G CARBS | 28.7G SUGARS | TRACE SALT | 9.3G FIBRE | 15G PROTEIN

STRAWBERRY BREAKFAST DIP

This light and summery breakfast is rich in calcium, vitamin C and antioxidants, and can be prepared in advance and stored in the refrigerator.

SERVES: 4   PREP: 10 MINS   COOK: 5 MINS

100 g/3¹/2 oz strawberries, hulled and roughly
chopped, plus extra, halved, to decorate
200 g/7 oz natural fromage frais
1 tsp lemon juice
4 slices of wholegrain bread
2 nectarines, halved, stoned and cut into wedges

1   Put the strawberries in a blender and process to a purée, then pour into a mixing bowl. Stir in the fromage frais and lemon juice. Cover and chill in the refrigerator if you have time.

2   Toast the bread and cut it into fingers. Spoon the strawberry mixture into four bowls and place each on a plate. Arrange the nectarine wedges and toast fingers on the plate around the dip to use as dippers. Decorate the dip with halves of strawberries and serve immediately.

STRAWBERRY SUNSHINE

Natural sugars found in the strawberries and nectarines in this breakfast are absorbed by the body more slowly than those from a high-energy drink. Strawberries are an excellent source of vitamin C, manganese and fibre.

PER SERVING: 166 CALS | 5G FAT | 3G SAT FAT | 24G CARBS | 13G SUGARS | 0.4G SALT | 4G FIBRE | 6.5G PROTEIN

YOGURT WITH BLUEBERRIES, HONEY AND NUTS

*Greek yogurt topped with fresh berries, honey and nuts
is quick to make and a delicious breakfast treat.*

SERVES: 4
PREP: 10 MINS, PLUS CHILLING   COOK: 5 MINS

3 tbsp runny honey
85 g/3 oz mixed unsalted nuts
125 g/4¹/2 oz Greek-style natural yogurt
200 g/7 oz blueberries

1   Heat the honey in a small saucepan over a medium heat. Stir in the nuts until well coated. Remove from the heat and leave to cool slightly.

2   Spoon the yogurt into four bowls, then spoon over the nuts and blueberries. Serve immediately.

SAY YES TO YOGURT

Yogurt is an excellent source of calcium. It is also packed with high-quality protein, magnesium and a variety of vitamins. Live yogurt, containing probiotics, has extra benefits, as these live in your digestive tract and help in the fight against infection.

PER SERVING: 237 CALS | 12.9G FAT | 2.7G SAT FAT | 27G CARBS | 19.3G SUGARS | TRACE SALT | 3.1G FIBRE | 7.3G PROTEIN

MANGO AND KALE JUICE

Mango's natural sweetness balances the kale in this health-boosting juice, and its perfumed flavour makes it refreshing as well as delicious.

SERVES: 1   PREP: 10 MINS

1 tbsp sesame seeds
juice of ½ lime
30 g/1 oz green curly kale, torn into pieces
1 mango, stoned, peeled and roughly chopped
225 ml/8 fl oz unsweetened rice, almond or soya milk
small handful of crushed ice

1 Put the sesame seeds in a blender and process to a fine powder. Add the lime juice, kale and mango and process until blended.

2 Add the milk and crushed ice and process again, until smooth. Pour into a glass and serve immediately.

KALE KICK-START

Kale boasts lots of calcium, C and B-group vitamins and beta-carotene. The antioxidant lutein helps protect the eyes against macular eye degeneration, while indoles offer protection against oestrogen-related cancers, and sulforaphane may help boost the liver's ability to detox carcinogenic compounds.

PER SERVING: 347 CALS | 9.9G FAT | 1.5G SAT FAT | 57.7G CARBS | 46.4G SUGARS | 0.1G SALT | 8.5G FIBRE | 12.9G PROTEIN

AVOCADO AND FRUIT JUICE

Protect your body from the inside out with this fresh, fruity drink that is bursting with antioxidants.

SERVES: 1   PREP: 10 MINS

½ avocado, stoned, peeled and roughly chopped
115 g/4 oz blueberries
115 g/4 oz strawberries, hulled
juice of 1 tangerine or small orange
125 ml/4 fl oz cold water
small handful of crushed ice (optional)

1 Put the avocado, blueberries, strawberries, tangerine juice and water in a blender and process until blended.

2 Add the crushed ice, if using, and process again until smooth. Pour into a glass and serve.

GOOD·FOR·YOU ORANGES

Oranges contain high concentrations of vitamin C, vitamin A, antioxidants, flavonoids, potassium, calcium, magnesium and fibre. They are also thought to help prevent some cancers.

PER SERVING: 250 CALS | 15G FAT | 3.5G SAT FAT | 18G CARBS | 18G SUGARS | TRACE SALT | 6G FIBRE | 3G PROTEIN

LUNCHES AND SNACKS

CEVICHE

Tangy and tongue-tinglingly good! The fish must be super-fresh for this Mexican favourite, which is bursting with chilli and sweet and sour flavours.

SERVES: 4   PREP: 30 MINS   CHILL: 1½ HOURS

2 ruby grapefruits
200 g/7 oz sea bass fillets, skinned, pin-boned and cut into cubes
300 g/10½ oz trout fillets, skinned, pin-boned and cut into cubes
finely grated zest and juice of 2 limes
1 red chilli, deseeded and finely chopped
½ red onion, finely chopped
1 tbsp virgin olive oil
15 g/½ oz fresh coriander, finely chopped
60 g/2¼ oz mixed baby spinach, watercress and rocket salad
salt and pepper

1 Cut the peel and pith away from the grapefruits with a small serrated knife. Hold each one above a bowl and cut between the membranes to release the segments. Squeeze the juice from the membranes into the bowl.

2 Put the sea bass and trout in a china or glass bowl, sprinkle over the lime zest and juice and chilli, then add the red onion, grapefruit segments and juice and oil. Season well with salt and pepper, then gently stir so all the fish is evenly coated in the lime juice.

3 Cover and chill in the refrigerator for 1–1½ hours, or until the fish has taken on a cooked appearance, with the sea bass bright white and the trout a paler, even-coloured pink.

4 Add the coriander and stir gently. Arrange the mixed leaf salad on four plates and spoon the ceviche on top, then serve immediately.

COOL CITRUS

Citrus fruits such as limes, oranges and grapefruits are bursting with vitamin C. This is a highly unstable vitamin, which is destroyed by heat, so try to eat them raw. It is needed daily for healthy gums and teeth, healing wounds and the production of collagen. Eating vitamin C-rich fruits with iron-rich spinach, watercress and rocket enables the body to absorb more of the iron.

PER SERVING: 209 CALS | 7.8G FAT | 1.3G SAT FAT | 13.5G CARBS | 10.8G SUGARS | 0.9G SALT | 2.2G FIBRE | 21.2G PROTEIN

LENTIL AND SPINACH SOUP

A beautifully fresh, light and fragrant soup that's easy to make and packed with nutrients.

SERVES: 4   PREP: 15 MINS   COOK: 45 MINS

1 tsp vegetable oil
1 onion, finely chopped
2 garlic cloves, finely chopped
2 celery sticks, finely chopped
200 g/7 oz carrots, finely chopped
1/2 tsp chilli powder
1 tsp smoked paprika
1 tsp cumin seeds
200 g/7 oz red lentils, washed
1 litre/1³/4 pints vegetable stock
50 g/1³/4 oz spinach, de-stalked and roughly chopped
100 g/3¹/2 oz cherry tomatoes, halved
salt and pepper
4 tbsp natural yogurt, to serve (optional)
4 pittas, cut into slices, to serve (optional)

1   Heat the oil in a large saucepan over a medium heat. Add the onion, garlic, celery and carrots and cook for 4–5 minutes, or until starting to soften.

2   Add the chilli powder, paprika and cumin seeds and cook for 1 minute, stirring constantly.

3   Add the red lentils and stock, then season with salt and pepper. Bring to the boil, then cook for 10 minutes. Cover and reduce the heat to low, then simmer gently for 20–25 minutes more, or until the vegetables and lentils are cooked.

4   Add the spinach and tomatoes and cook for 5 minutes more, or until the spinach has wilted. Taste and season again if needed. Serve in four bowls, with a tablespoon of yogurt in each bowl and the pittas, if using.

LOVELY LENTILS

Lentils are a good source of protein and rich in fibre. It is thought they can help reduce bad cholesterol and stabilize blood sugar levels, so slowing down the rate at which sugar is absorbed by the body.

PER SERVING: 255 CALS | 4.3G FAT | 1.5G SAT FAT | 43.1G CARBS | 7.9G SUGARS | 3.3G SALT | 8.9G FIBRE | 15.3G PROTEIN

SWEET RED PEPPER AND TOMATO SOUP

This warming and comforting soup is brimming with health-boosting, antioxidant-rich vegetables.

SERVES: 4   PREP: 10 MINS   COOK: 35 MINS

1 tbsp olive oil
2 tbsp cold water
2 red peppers, deseeded and finely chopped
1 garlic clove, finely chopped
1 onion, finely chopped
400 g/14 oz canned chopped tomatoes
1.2 litres/2 pints vegetable stock
salt and pepper
fresh basil leaves, to garnish

1 Put the oil, water, peppers, garlic and onion in a saucepan over a medium–low heat and cook for 5–10 minutes, or until all the vegetables have softened. Cover and simmer for 10 minutes.

2 Add the tomatoes and stock and season with salt and pepper. Simmer, uncovered, for 15 minutes. Serve garnished with basil leaves.

RED PEPPER BOOST

All peppers are rich in vitamins A, C and K, but red peppers are simply bursting with them. Antioxidant vitamins A and C help to prevent cell damage, cancer and diseases related to ageing, and support immune function. They also reduce inflammation such as that found in arthritis and asthma.

PER SERVING: 97 CALS | 5.4G FAT | 1.7G SAT FAT | 12.8G CARBS | 7.1G SUGARS | 3.6G SALT | 3.2G FIBRE | 2.2G PROTEIN

PRAWN-FILLED SWEET JACKET POTATOES

We all love jacket potatoes, and this healthy lunch is topped with low-fat cottage cheese, an antioxidant-boosting mango and corn salsa and protein-powered prawns.

SERVES: 4   PREP: 5 MINS   COOK: 1 HOUR

4 x 250 g/9 oz sweet potatoes, scrubbed and pricked with a fork
85 g/3 oz frozen sweetcorn
125 g/4 1/2 oz plum tomatoes, cut into cubes
4 spring onions, finely chopped
1 mango, stoned, peeled and cut into cubes
15 g/1/2 oz fresh coriander, finely chopped
1 red chilli, deseeded and finely chopped (optional)
300 g/10 1/2 oz cooked and peeled prawns
finely grated zest and juice of 1 lime
300 g/10 1/2 oz low-fat cottage cheese
salt and pepper

1 Preheat the oven to 200°C/400°F/Gas Mark 6. Put the sweet potatoes on a baking tray and bake for 1 hour, or until they feel soft when gently squeezed.

2 Meanwhile, bring a saucepan of water to the boil, add the frozen sweetcorn and cook for 3 minutes, or until tender. Drain into a sieve, then rinse under cold running water.

3 Put the tomatoes, spring onions and mango in a bowl, then stir in the coriander, red chilli, if using, and sweetcorn and season with salt and pepper. Cover and chill in the refrigerator.

4 Put the prawns and lime zest and juice in another bowl and season with salt and pepper. Cover and chill in the refrigerator.

5 Put the potatoes on a serving plate, slit them in half, then open them out. Top with spoonfuls of the cottage cheese, then fill with the salsa and prawns.

SUPER SPRING ONIONS

Spring onions are small, immature plants of the onion family. Because they are leafy greens, they contain more plant-derived antioxidants and fibre than onions and shallots. They contain A, C and B-group vitamins, and are a rich source of vitamin K.

PER SERVING: 407 CALS | 2.3G FAT | 0.7G SAT FAT | 73.4G CARBS | 27.2G SUGARS | 2.1G SALT | 10.2G FIBRE | 25.5G PROTEIN

QUINOA SALAD WITH FENNEL AND ORANGE

Fennel is known to be an effective diuretic and calms the stomach, so it is a useful addition to any detox diet. It is delicious with zingy orange.

SERVES: 4   PREP: 20 MINS   COOK: 15 MINS

900 ml/1½ pints vegetable stock
225 g/8 oz quinoa, rinsed
3 oranges
250 g/9 oz fennel, thinly sliced using a mandolin, green feathery tops reserved and torn into small pieces
2 spring onions, finely chopped
15 g/½ oz fresh flat-leaf parsley, roughly chopped

DRESSING
juice of ½ lemon
3 tbsp virgin olive oil
pepper

1   Bring the stock to the boil in a saucepan, add the quinoa and simmer for 10–12 minutes, or until the germs separate from the seeds. Drain off the stock and discard, then spoon the quinoa into a salad bowl and leave to cool.

2   Grate the zest from two of the oranges and put it in a jam jar. Cut the peel and pith away from all three oranges with a small serrated knife. Hold each one above a bowl and cut between the membranes to release the segments. Squeeze the juice from the membranes into the jam jar.

3   Add the orange segments, fennel slices, spring onions and parsley to the quinoa.

4   To make the dressing, add the lemon juice and oil to the jam jar, season to taste with pepper, screw on the lid and shake well. Drizzle the dressing over the salad and toss. Garnish with the fennel fronds and serve immediately.

NUTRITIOUS QUINOA

Quinoa, pronounced 'keen-wa', contains all eight essential amino acids, plus it's rich in fibre and minerals and lower in carbs than most grains.

PER SERVING: 388 CALS | 8.3G FAT | 1.9G SAT FAT | 54G CARBS | 11.6G SUGARS | 2.1G SALT | 8.4G FIBRE | 10G PROTEIN

VIETNAMESE TOFU AND NOODLE SALAD

Packed with protein-boosting tofu and baby green edamame beans, this gingered salad is mixed with buckwheat noodles, making it a superfood feast.

SERVES: 4
PREP: 15 MINS, PLUS MARINATING   COOK: 8 MINS

400 g/14 oz firm chilled tofu, drained and cut into 8 slices
115 g/4 oz buckwheat soba noodles
200 g/7 oz frozen edamame beans
1 carrot, cut into matchstick strips
85 g/3 oz mangetout, cut into matchstick strips
115 g/4 oz rainbow chard, stems cut into matchstick strips, leaves thinly shredded
15 g/1/2 oz fresh coriander, roughly chopped

MARINADE
2 tbsp tamari sauce or soy sauce
2 tbsp sesame seeds
1 red chilli, deseeded and finely chopped (optional)
4-cm/1¹/2-inch piece fresh ginger, peeled and finely chopped

DRESSING
4 tbsp virgin rapeseed oil
juice of 1/2 lemon
1 tbsp sweet chilli dipping sauce

1   Line the base of the grill pan with foil. Arrange the tofu on the grill pan in a single layer and fold up the edges of the foil to make a dish.

2   To make the marinade, mix together the tamari sauce, sesame seeds, chilli, if using, and half the ginger in a small bowl. Spoon this over the tofu, then leave to marinate for 10 minutes.

3   Bring a large saucepan of water to the boil, add the noodles and frozen edamame beans and cook for 3–4 minutes, or until just tender. Drain into a sieve, then rinse under cold running water.

4   Put the carrot, mangetout, rainbow chard stems and leaves and coriander in a large salad bowl. Add the noodles and edamame beans and gently toss.

5   To make the dressing, put the oil, lemon juice, sweet chilli dipping sauce and remaining ginger in a bowl and whisk with a fork. Pour over the salad and gently toss.

6   Preheat the grill to medium–high. Turn the tofu over in the marinade, then grill for 2 minutes on each side, or until browned. Leave to cool for a few minutes, then cut into cubes and sprinkle over the salad with any remaining marinade and serve.

TERRIFIC TOFU

An everyday ingredient in Chinese and Thai cooking, tofu is made in much the same way as we make cheese, but using soya milk. It is rich in protein, vitamin E, calcium, iron and other minerals, but low in fat. It is believed to alleviate the symptoms of the menopause, and help protect against heart disease.

PER SERVING: 483 CALS | 27.2G FAT | 2.6G SAT FAT | 34.5G CARBS | 6.1G SUGARS | 2.6G SALT | 8.3G FIBRE | 28.8G PROTEIN

ROAST BEETROOT AND SQUASH SALAD

This nutty-tasting wholegrain salad, topped with two superfoods — beetroot and butternut squash — can be made the night before, chilled, then tossed with beetroot leaves to serve.

SERVES: 4   PREP: 25 MINS   COOK: 30 MINS

5 raw beetroot (approx 450 g/1 lb), cut into cubes
450 g/1 lb butternut squash flesh, cut into cubes
4 tbsp virgin olive oil
100 g/3¹/2 oz brown basmati rice
100 g/3¹/2 oz red Camargue rice
100 g/3¹/2 oz quick-cook farro
115 g/4 oz baby beetroot leaves
salt and pepper

DRESSING
1 tbsp flaxseed oil
2 tbsp red wine vinegar
¹/2 tsp smoked hot paprika
1 tsp fennel seeds, roughly crushed
2 tsp tomato purée

1 Preheat the oven to 200°C/400°F/Gas Mark 6. Put the beetroot and squash in a roasting tin, drizzle with half the olive oil and season with salt and pepper. Roast for 30 minutes, or until just tender.

2 Meanwhile, bring a large saucepan of water to the boil, add the basmati and red Camargue rice and cook, uncovered, for 15 minutes. Add the farro and cook for 10 minutes more, or until all the grains are tender. Drain and rinse, then transfer to a platter.

3 To make the dressing, put all the ingredients and the remaining 2 tablespoons of olive oil in a jam jar, season to taste with salt and pepper, screw on the lid and shake well. Drizzle over the rice mixture, then toss gently together.

4 Spoon the roasted vegetables over the grains and leave to cool. Toss gently, then sprinkle with the beetroot leaves and serve immediately.

BEETROOT BONANZA

Packed with vitamins, minerals, protein, energy-boosting carbs and powerful antioxidants, beetroot is thought to help reduce the oxidation of LDL cholesterol, so reducing the risk of heart disease and stroke. Rich in potassium, folic acid and iron, it can help prevent tiredness and may even slow the progression of dementia.

PER SERVING: 505 CALS | 19.3G FAT | 2.5G SAT FAT | 75G CARBS | 10.7G SUGARS | 1.1G SALT | 9G FIBRE | 10G PROTEIN

SUPER GREEN SALAD

Super-charged with vitamins and minerals, this crisp green salad tastes delicious with the addition of creamy smooth avocado and crunchy toasted seeds.

SERVES: 4   PREP: 15 MINS   COOK: 5 MINS

2 tbsp pumpkin seeds
2 tbsp sunflower seeds
2 tbsp sesame seeds
4 tsp tamari sauce or soy sauce
250 g/9 oz broccoli, cut into florets
85 g/3 oz baby spinach
55 g/2 oz kale, thinly shredded
15 g/1/2 oz fresh coriander, roughly chopped
2 avocados, stoned, peeled and sliced
juice of 2 limes

DRESSING
3 tbsp flaxseed oil
2 tsp runny honey
pepper

1 Place a frying pan over a high heat. Add the pumpkin, sunflower and sesame seeds, cover and dry-fry for 3–4 minutes, or until lightly toasted and beginning to pop, shaking the pan from time to time. Remove from the heat and stir in the tamari sauce.

2 Half-fill the base of a steamer with water, bring to the boil, then put the broccoli in the steamer top, cover with a lid and steam for 3–5 minutes, or until tender. Transfer to a salad bowl and add the spinach, kale and coriander.

3 Put the avocados and half the lime juice in a small bowl and toss well, then tip them into the salad bowl.

4 To make the dressing, put the remaining lime juice, the oil, honey and a little pepper in a small jug and fork together. Sprinkle the toasted seeds over the salad and serve immediately with the dressing for pouring over.

GO GREEN

Spinach, kale and broccoli contain beneficial phytochemicals that help to prevent carcinogens from damaging DNA and so help to prevent against cancer. They are also rich in vitamins A and C, B vitamins and iron.

PER SERVING: 388 CALS | 32.8G FAT | 3.9G SAT FAT | 22.1G CARBS | 5G SUGARS | 0.9G SALT | 10.7G FIBRE | 9G PROTEIN

CRANBERRY AND RED CABBAGE COLESLAW

Forget about coleslaw coated in thick, high-calorie mayonnaise. This version is tossed with a tangy orange and olive oil dressing flavoured with chia seeds and toasted walnuts.

SERVES: 4   PREP: 15 MINS   COOK: 3 MINS

150 g/5$\frac{1}{2}$ oz red cabbage, thinly shredded
1 carrot, coarsely grated
140 g/5 oz cauliflower, cut into florets
1 red-skinned dessert apple, quartered, cored and very thinly sliced
40 g/1$\frac{1}{2}$ oz dried cranberries
50 g/1$\frac{3}{4}$ oz alfalfa and sango radish shoots

DRESSING
50 g/1$\frac{3}{4}$ oz walnuts, roughly chopped
juice of 1 orange
4 tbsp virgin olive oil
2 tbsp chia seeds
salt and pepper

1   Put the red cabbage, carrot and cauliflower in a salad bowl. Add the apple, dried cranberries and shoots and toss well.

2   To make the dressing, put the walnuts in a large frying pan and toast for 2–3 minutes, or until just beginning to brown.

3   Put the orange juice, oil and chia seeds in a small bowl, season with salt and pepper, then stir in the hot walnuts. Pour the dressing over the salad and toss. Serve immediately or cover and chill in the refrigerator until needed.

HEALTHY CRANBERRIES

Cranberries are jam-packed with antioxidants. They are believed to help reduce inflammation and to be a useful tool in the fight against heart disease.

PER SERVING: 320 CALS | 23.2G FAT | 2.8G SAT FAT | 29.5G CARBS | 16G SUGARS | 0.8G SALT | 9.3G FIBRE | 4.9G PROTEIN

SWEET POTATO FRIES

A sunshine snack, Caribbean-style. Replace the oil spray with vegetable oil if you prefer, but heat it in the oven before adding the sweet potatoes.

SERVES: 4   PREP: 15 MINS   COOK: 20 MINS

2 squirts of vegetable oil spray
900 g/2 lb sweet potatoes
1/2 tsp salt
1/2 tsp ground cumin
1/4 tsp cayenne pepper

1 Preheat the oven to 230°C/450°F/Gas Mark 8. Spray a large baking tray with vegetable oil spray.

2 Cut the sweet potatoes into 5-mm/1/4-inch thick chips. Arrange them on the prepared baking tray in a single layer and spray them with vegetable oil spray.

3 Mix together the salt, cumin and cayenne pepper in a small bowl, then sprinkle the mixture evenly over the sweet potatoes and toss well.

4 Bake for 15–20 minutes, or until cooked through and lightly coloured. Serve hot.

SWEET POTATOES

Loaded with vitamins A and C, fibre and potassium, sweet potatoes are a terrific superfood. They also contain cancer-fighting antioxidants and useful amounts of magnesium and manganese.

PER SERVING: 194 CALS | 0.1G FAT | TRACE SAT FAT | 45.2 CARBS | 9.4G SUGARS | 1G SALT | 6.7G FIBRE | 3.5G PROTEIN

GUACAMOLE DIP

A Mexican-style dip that is delicious with raw, nutrition-packed vegetable crudités and hot pitta breads.

SERVES: 4   PREP: 10 MINS

2 large avocados, stoned, peeled and sliced
juice of 2 limes
2 large garlic cloves, crushed
1 tsp mild chilli powder, plus extra to garnish
salt and pepper

1 Put the avocado slices, lime juice, garlic and chilli in a food processor and process until smooth. Season with salt and pepper.

2 Transfer to a serving bowl, garnish with chilli powder and serve immediately.

AMAZING AVOCADOS

Avocados are high in vitamin C and potassium, and contain healthy monounsaturated fats. They are an excellent source of vitamin E, which helps keep the heart healthy, and contain good amounts of vitamin B6, which is essential for a healthy nervous system.

PER SERVING: 170 CALS | 14.7G FAT | 2.1G SAT FAT | 11.1G CARBS | 1.1G SUGARS | 0.8G SALT | 7.1G FIBRE | 2.3G PROTEIN

POWER BALLS

Packed with superfoods, these truffle-sized balls are a mighty mixture of slow-release carbohydrates, protein and minerals. They're great for lunch boxes in place of chocolate.

MAKES: 20 BALLS   PREP: 25 MINS

85 g/3 oz 70% plain chocolate
40 g/1½ oz sunflower seeds
40 g/1½ oz flaxseeds
40 g/1½ oz sesame seeds
100 g/3½ oz Brazil nuts, roughly chopped
140 g/5 oz Medjool dates, stoned
40 g/1½ oz goji berries
1 tsp ground cinnamon
1 tbsp maca (see page 16)
40 g/1½ oz unsweetened desiccated coconut
6 tbsp maple syrup

1 Break 55 g/2 oz chocolate into pieces and reserve the rest. Put the sunflower seeds, flaxseeds, sesame seeds, Brazil nuts and chocolate in a food processor and process until finely ground, scraping down the sides of the processor once or twice.

2 Add the dates, goji berries, cinnamon, maca and 25 g/1 oz coconut, then spoon in the maple syrup. Process until you have a coarse paste.

3 Using a measuring spoon, scoop out tablespoons of the mixture onto a plate, then adjust the sizes of the mounds to make 20. Roll them into balls.

4 Put the remaining coconut on one plate and finely grate the remaining chocolate onto another plate. Roll half the balls in the coconut and the rest in the chocolate. Pack into an airtight container and store in the fridge for up to three days.

DATES FOR FIBRE

Dates are high in fibre, and are a good source of potassium, calcium, iron, phosphorus, manganese, copper and magnesium. They are thought to help prevent some cancers and intestinal diseases.

PER BALL: 132 CALS | 7.7G FAT | 2.4G SAT FAT | 15.2G CARBS | 10.9G SUGARS | TRACE SALT | 2.4G FIBRE | 2.1G PROTEIN

HONEY AND BLUEBERRY BARS

Honey gives cakes and traybakes a rich flavour and chewy texture.
These portable snacks are ideal for packing ahead of a long journey.

MAKES: 12 BARS
PREP: 15 MINS COOK: 30 MINS, PLUS COOLING

sunflower oil, to grease
85 g/3 oz self-raising flour
55 g/2 oz quinoa flakes
55 g/2 oz puffed rice
55 g/2 oz flaked almonds
225 g/8 oz blueberries
100 g/3½ oz butter
100 g/3½ oz runny honey
1 egg, beaten

1 Preheat the oven to 180°C/350°F/Gas Mark 4. Brush a shallow 28 x 18-cm/11 x 7-inch baking tin with oil and line the base with baking paper.

2 Mix together the flour, quinoa flakes, puffed rice, almonds and blueberries in a bowl.

3 Heat the butter and honey in a saucepan over a low heat until melted, then pour over the dry ingredients, add the egg and stir well.

4 Spoon the mixture into the prepared tin and level with a spatula. Bake for 25–30 minutes, or until golden brown and firm. Leave to cool in the tin for 15 minutes, then cut into 12 bars and transfer to a wire rack to cool completely.

HEAVENLY HONEY

Honey is a natural sweetener which has long been praised for its antibacterial properties.

PER BAR: 182 CALS | 9.3G FAT | 1.6G SAT FAT | 22.9G CARBS | 9.2G SUGARS | 0.1G SALT | 1.5G FIBRE | 3G PROTEIN

MAINS

Beef stir-fry	74
Pork medallions with pomegranate salad	76
Jerk chicken with papaya and avocado salsa	78
Spicy roast turkey	80
Tangy turkey meatballs with edamame beans	82
Grilled trout stuffed with spinach and mushrooms	85
Gingered salmon with stir-fried kale	86
Grilled salmon with mango and lime salsa	88
Risotto primavera	90
Beetroot burgers in buns	93
Stuffed red peppers	94
Black bean and quinoa burritos	97
Raw shoots and seeds super salad	98

BEEF STIR-FRY

Beef is high in iron and the vegetables in this dish are rich in vitamin C, which helps us to absorb the iron, making it a great combination!

SERVES: 2   PREP: 10 MINS   COOK: 12 MINS

2 tsp olive oil

140 g/5 oz beef steak, such as topside, visible fat removed, cut into thin strips

1 orange pepper, deseeded and cut into thin strips

4 spring onions, finely chopped

1–2 fresh jalapeño chillies, deseeded and thinly sliced

2 garlic cloves, finely chopped

115 g/4 oz mangetout, halved diagonally

115 g/4 oz large field mushrooms, sliced

2 tsp hoisin sauce

1 tbsp orange juice

85 g/3 oz rocket or watercress

4 tbsp sweet chilli sauce, to serve (optional)

1 Heat the oil in a wok over a medium–high heat for 30 seconds. Add the beef and stir-fry for 1 minute, or until browned. Transfer to a plate with a slotted spoon.

2 Add the orange pepper, spring onions, jalapeño chillies and garlic to the wok and stir-fry for 2 minutes. Add the mangetout and mushrooms and stir-fry for 2 minutes more.

3 Return the beef to the wok. Add the hoisin sauce and orange juice and stir-fry for 2–3 minutes, or until the beef is cooked and the vegetables are tender but still firm. Add the rocket and stir-fry until it starts to wilt. Serve immediately, with a small bowl of sweet chilli sauce, if using.

GREAT GARLIC

Garlic is considered to have anti-inflammatory properties, as well as antibacterial and antiviral benefits. It is believed to help lower cholesterol and blood pressure.

PER SERVING: 160 CALS | 3G FAT | 1G SAT FAT | 9G CARBS | 8G SUGARS | 0.8G SALT | 5G FIBRE | 20G PROTEIN

PORK MEDALLIONS WITH POMEGRANATE SALAD

*Fresh herbs and jewel-like pomegranate give this nutritious salad
a delicious Middle Eastern flavour.*

SERVES: 4   PREP: 10 MINS   COOK: 30 MINS

150 g/5¹/2 oz wheatberries
25 g/1 oz fresh flat-leaf parsley, roughly chopped
55 g/2 oz kale, thinly shredded
seeds of 1 pomegranate
1 tbsp olive oil
500 g/1 lb 2 oz pork medallions, visible fat removed
2 garlic cloves, finely chopped
salt and pepper

DRESSING
50 g/1¾ oz walnuts, roughly chopped
3 tbsp virgin olive oil
3 tsp pomegranate molasses
juice of 1 lemon

1 Bring a medium saucepan of water to the boil. Add the wheatberries and simmer for 25–30 minutes, or until tender. Drain and rinse.

2 Meanwhile, to make the dressing, put the walnuts in a large frying pan and toast for 2–3 minutes, or until just beginning to brown. Put the virgin olive oil, the pomegranate molasses and lemon juice in a small bowl and mix together with a fork. Season with salt and pepper and stir in the hot walnuts.

3 Mix together the parsley, kale and pomegranate seeds in a large bowl.

4 Heat the olive oil in the frying pan over a medium heat. Add the pork and garlic, season with salt and pepper, and fry for 10 minutes, turning halfway through, until browned and cooked. Cut into the centre of one of the pork medallions; any juices that run out should be clear and piping hot with steam rising. Slice the pork into strips.

5 Add the wheatberries to the kale and gently toss. Transfer to a platter, pour over the dressing, then top with the pork.

PREPARING POMEGRANATES

Cut through the hard outer casing of a pomegranate to reveal the closely-packed ruby seeds that are rich in vitamins A, C and E plus antioxidants. Break and flex the fruit to pop out the seeds or turn upside-down over a bowl and hit the rounded edge with a wooden spoon to bash them out.

PER SERVING: 540 CALS | 29.7G FAT | 5.2G SAT FAT | 37G CARBS | 4.5G SUGARS | 0.9G SALT | 6.9G FIBRE | 34.6G PROTEIN

JERK CHICKEN WITH PAPAYA AND AVOCADO SALSA

Glazed chicken needn't have a high-calorie coating,
as this flavour-packed Jamaican dry spice rub shows.

SERVES: 4   PREP: 15 MINS   COOK: 35 MINS

1 kg/2 lb 4 oz small chicken drumsticks, skinned
1 tbsp olive oil
1 cos lettuce, leaves separated and torn into pieces (optional)
85 g/3 oz baby spinach (optional)

JERK SPICE RUB
1 tsp allspice berries, crushed
1 tsp coriander seeds, crushed
1 tsp mild paprika
1/4 tsp freshly grated nutmeg
1 tbsp fresh thyme leaves
1 tbsp black peppercorns, coarsely crushed
pinch of salt

PAPAYA AND AVOCADO SALSA
1 papaya, halved, deseeded, peeled and cut into cubes
2 large avocados, stoned, peeled and cut into cubes
finely grated zest and juice of 1 lime
1/2 red chilli, deseeded and finely chopped
1/2 red onion, finely chopped
15 g/1/2 oz fresh coriander, finely chopped
2 tsp chia seeds

1   Preheat the oven to 200°C/400°F/Gas Mark 6. To make the jerk spice rub, mix together all the ingredients in a small bowl.

2   Slash each chicken drumstick two or three times with a knife, then put them in a roasting tin and drizzle with the oil. Sprinkle the spice mix over the chicken, then rub it in with your fingers, washing your hands well afterwards. Roast the chicken for 30–35 minutes, or until browned with piping hot juices that run clear with no sign of pink when a knife is inserted into the thickest part of a drumstick.

3   Meanwhile, to make the salsa, put the papaya and avocados in a bowl, sprinkle over the lime zest and juice, then toss well. Add the chilli, red onion, coriander and chia seeds and stir.

4   Toss the lettuce and spinach together, if using. Serve with the chicken and salsa.

THREE CHEERS FOR CHIA

Chia is a good source of Omega-3 fats and fibre, and contains calcium, manganese and phosphorus. It is thought to have many health benefits, including providing energy, stabilizing blood sugar, aiding digestion and lowering cholesterol.

PER SERVING: 394 CALS | 18.1G FAT | 3.2G SAT FAT | 17.1G CARBS | 5.4G SUGARS | 0.9G SALT | 7.8G FIBRE | 42G PROTEIN

SPICY ROAST TURKEY

This easy one-pan dish makes a quick and healthy mid-week supper –
with very little washing up required!

SERVES: 4   PREP: 20 MINS   COOK: 45 MINS

3 tbsp olive oil
500 g/1 lb 2 oz pumpkin or butternut squash, deseeded, peeled and cut into large pieces
400 g/14 oz sweet potatoes, cut into large pieces
200 g/7 oz baby carrots, tops trimmed, larger ones halved lengthways
1 small cauliflower, cut into large florets
450 g/1 lb skinless and boneless turkey breast, cut into 1.5-cm/1/2-inch-thick slices
salt and pepper

SPICE BLEND

2 tbsp sesame seeds
2 tbsp sunflower seeds
2 tsp mild paprika
1 tsp coriander seeds, crushed
1 tsp fennel seeds, crushed
1 tsp cumin seeds, crushed

1 Preheat the oven to 200°C/400°F/Gas Mark 6. Pour the oil into a large roasting tin, then heat in the oven for 5 minutes.

2 Meanwhile, to make the spice blend, mix all the ingredients together in a small bowl and season with salt and pepper.

3 Put the pumpkin, sweet potatoes and carrots in the roasting tin and toss in the hot oil. Roast for 15 minutes.

4 Add the cauliflower to the roasting tin and turn all the vegetables so they are coated in the oil. Push them to the edges of the tin, then add the turkey in a single layer.

5 Sprinkle the spice blend over the turkey and vegetables, then turn the vegetables so they are evenly coated. Roast for 20–25 minutes, or until the vegetables are tender, and the turkey is golden brown with piping hot juices that run clear with no sign of pink when the thickest slice is cut in half.

6 Spoon the turkey and vegetables onto plates and serve immediately.

TALKING TURKEY

Turkey is a rich source of protein, but is low in fat. It also contains iron, zinc, potassium and phosphorus, as well as vitamin B6 and niacin, which are essential for the body's energy production.

PER SERVING: 455 CALS | 16.6G FAT | 2.3G SAT FAT | 45.5G CARBS | 11G SUGARS | 1.1G SALT | 9.8G FIBRE | 34.2G PROTEIN

TANGY TURKEY MEATBALLS WITH EDAMAME BEANS

Minced turkey breast can be quickly blitzed together with lemon and garlic to make this simple mid-week supper that's super-healthy, low in fat and high in protein.

SERVES: 4   PREP: 20 MINS   COOK: 30 MINS

250 g/9 oz short-grain brown rice
1 small onion, roughly chopped
1 slice of wholemeal bread, torn into pieces
2 garlic cloves, thinly sliced
500 g/1 lb 2 oz minced turkey breast
finely grated zest of 1 unwaxed lemon
1 tbsp olive oil
350 ml/12 fl oz chicken stock
175 g/6 oz frozen edamame beans
115 g/4 oz peas
2 egg yolks
15 g/½ oz fresh flat-leaf parsley, roughly chopped
15 g/½ oz fresh mint, roughly chopped
salt and pepper

1 Cook the rice in a large pan of lightly salted boiling water for 30 minutes, or until tender. Drain well.

2 Meanwhile, put the onion, bread and garlic in a food processor and process until finely chopped. Add the turkey and lemon zest and season with salt and pepper, then process again briefly until mixed.

3 Spoon the mixture into 20 mounds on a chopping board, then squeeze them into balls using wet hands.

4 Heat the oil in a large lidded frying pan over a medium heat. Add the meatballs in a single layer and fry for 15 minutes, or until evenly golden, turning from time to time.

5 Add the stock, cover and cook for 5 minutes. Add the edamame beans and peas, re-cover and cook for 5 minutes more, or until the vegetables are just tender and the meatballs are cooked through with juices that are piping hot and that run clear with no sign of pink when a meatball is cut in half. Remove from the heat and spoon the stock into a jug.

6 Meanwhile, whisk the egg yolks together in a large bowl and season with salt and pepper. Gradually whisk in the stock until smooth, then pour the mixture back into the pan. Place over a low heat and cook, stirring all the time, for 3–4 minutes, or until thickened. Be careful not to have the heat too high or the egg yolks will scramble.

7 Stir in the herbs. Spoon the rice into shallow bowls, top with the meatballs and sauce, and serve immediately.

BRILLIANT BROWN RICE

Brown rice is unrefined, so it still has the hull and bran, making it rich in fibre, B vitamins, magnesium and potassium.

PER SERVING: 546 CALS | 11.8G FAT | 2.4G SAT FAT | 62.4G CARBS | 3.4G SUGARS | 1.8G SALT | 6.5G FIBRE | 45G PROTEIN

GRILLED TROUT STUFFED WITH SPINACH AND MUSHROOMS

This glamorous-looking dish is a great way to power-up on Omega-3-rich oily fish while enjoying a delicious dinner for two!

SERVES: 2   PREP: 30 MINS   COOK: 20 MINS

2 x 350 g/12 oz trout, gutted and fins removed
1 tbsp vegetable oil
400 g/14 oz new potatoes, boiled (optional)
salt and pepper

STUFFING

25 g/1 oz butter
2 shallots, finely chopped
55 g/2 oz mushrooms, finely chopped
55 g/2 oz baby spinach
1 tbsp chopped fresh flat-leaf parsley or tarragon
finely grated zest of 1 unwaxed lemon
grating of fresh nutmeg

TOMATO SALSA

2 tomatoes, peeled, deseeded and finely chopped
10-cm/4-inch piece of cucumber, finely chopped
2 spring onions, finely chopped
1 tbsp olive oil

1 Rinse the trout inside and out under cold running water, then pat dry with kitchen paper. Slash the skin of each fish on both sides about five times with a knife. Brush with the oil and season well inside and out with salt and pepper.

2 To make the stuffing, melt the butter in a small saucepan over a medium–low heat. Add the shallots and fry for 2–3 minutes. Add the mushrooms and fry for 2 minutes. Add the spinach and cook for 2–3 minutes, or until it has just wilted. Remove from the heat and stir in the parsley, lemon zest and a good grating of nutmeg. Leave to cool.

3 Preheat the grill to medium-high. Line the grill rack with foil. Fill the cavities of the trout with the mushroom and spinach stuffing, then re-shape them.

4 Grill the trout, turning halfway, for 10–12 minutes, or until the fish flakes easily when pressed with a knife.

5 Meanwhile, to make the tomato salsa, mix together all the ingredients and season well with salt and pepper.

6 Serve the trout with the salsa spooned over, with the new potatoes, if using.

TASTY TROUT

Trout is rich in 0mega–3 fatty acids, which studies show help to reduce the risk of heart disease and strokes.

PER SERVING: 551 CALS | 36.5G FAT | 11.2G SAT FAT | 13G CARBS | 4.4G SUGARS | 3.5G SALT | 3.1G FIBRE | 43.4G PROTEIN

GINGERED SALMON WITH STIR-FRIED KALE

A stir-fry is a great way of making sure you pack fresh vegetables into your diet, and this one is low in calories and carbohydrates.

SERVES: 4   PREP: 20 MINS   COOK: 10 MINS

4 x 150 g/5½ oz salmon steaks, skinned
5-cm/2-inch piece fresh ginger, peeled and finely chopped
3 garlic cloves, finely chopped
1 red chilli, deseeded and finely chopped
3 tbsp tamari sauce or soy sauce
200 g/7 oz broccoli, cut into florets
6 tbsp water
1 tbsp sunflower oil
1 large leek, sliced
115 g/4 oz kale, thinly shredded
2 tbsp Shaoxing wine
juice of 1 orange

1 Preheat the grill to medium–high and line the base of the grill pan with foil. Arrange the salmon on the grill pan and fold up the edges of the foil to make a dish. Sprinkle over half the ginger, half the garlic and half the chilli, then drizzle with 1 tablespoon of tamari sauce. Grill, turning once, for 8–10 minutes, or until browned and the fish flakes easily when pressed with a knife.

2 Meanwhile, put the broccoli and water in a wok or large frying pan, cover and cook over a medium–high heat for 3–4 minutes, or until the broccoli is almost tender. Pour off any remaining water.

3 Add the oil to the wok and increase the heat to high. When it is hot, add the leek, kale and the remaining ginger, garlic and chilli and stir-fry for 2–3 minutes, or until the kale has just wilted.

4 Mix in the remaining tamari sauce, the Shaoxing wine and orange juice and cook for 1 minute more. Spoon onto plates, break up a salmon steak over each plate and serve.

BROCCOLI BOOST

Broccoli is bursting with nutrition. It contains high levels of both fibre and vitamin C. It is also rich in vitamins A, K and B-group, iron, zinc, and phosphorus. Broccoli is a good source of phytonutrients, which are thought to help reduce the risk of diabetes and heart disease and protect against certain types of cancer.

PER SERVING: 348 CALS | 13.6G FAT | 1.9G SAT FAT | 21.8G CARBS | 6.3G SUGARS | 2.1G SALT | 3.5G FIBRE | 35.2G PROTEIN

GRILLED SALMON WITH MANGO AND LIME SALSA

The refreshing, zingy flavours of mango and lime complement the salmon perfectly in this superfood-packed meal.

SERVES: 4   PREP: 15 MINS   COOK: 10 MINS

2 tbsp lime juice
1 tbsp runny honey
2 tbsp chopped fresh dill
4 x 115 g/4 oz salmon fillets
salt and pepper
new potatoes, cooked, to serve (optional)
salad leaves, to serve

MANGO AND LIME SALSA

1 mango, stoned, peeled and cut into cubes
finely grated zest and juice of 1 lime
2 tbsp desiccated coconut

1 Preheat the grill to medium–high and line the grill rack with foil.

2 Put the lime juice, honey and half the dill in a wide bowl and mix well. Season to taste with salt and pepper. Add the salmon and turn to coat in the glaze. Arrange the salmon on the grill rack, then grill, turning once, for 8–10 minutes, or until browned and the fish flakes easily when pressed with a knife.

3 Meanwhile, to make the salsa, put the mango, lime zest and juice, desiccated coconut and remaining dill in a small bowl and mix well.

4 Serve the salmon, topped with the salsa, with the potatoes, if using, and salad leaves.

SUPER SALMON

Studies have found that people who eat oily fish such as salmon, herring, mackerel or sardines twice a week are less likely to suffer from heart disease or strokes. It is the omega-3 fatty acids in the fish that help to protect against heart and circulation problems.

PER SERVING: 290 CALS | 17.5G FAT | 6G SAT FAT | 10G CARBS | 9G SUGARS | 0.1G SALT | 3G FIBRE | 24G PROTEIN

RISOTTO PRIMAVERA

*Short-grain brown rice adds a nutty, moreish taste to risotto.
It's high in fibre, and is believed to help lower cholesterol.*

SERVES: 4   PREP: 20 MINS   COOK: 50 MINS

1.2 litres/2 pints vegetable stock
1 tbsp olive oil
1 large leek, thinly sliced, white and green slices kept separate
2 garlic cloves, finely chopped
250 g/9 oz short-grain brown rice
150 g/5$\frac{1}{2}$ oz baby carrots, tops trimmed, halved lengthways
100 g/3$\frac{1}{2}$ oz asparagus spears, woody stems removed
225 g/8 oz courgettes, cut into cubes
25 g/1 oz butter
70 g/2$\frac{1}{2}$ oz Parmesan cheese, finely grated
60 g/2$\frac{1}{4}$ oz mixed baby spinach, watercress and rocket leaves

1 Bring the stock to the boil in a saucepan.

2 Meanwhile, heat the oil in a large frying pan over a medium heat. Add the white leek slices and garlic and cook for 3–4 minutes, or until softened but not browned.

3 Stir in the rice and cook for 1 minute. Pour in half the hot stock, bring back to the boil, then cover and simmer for 15 minutes.

4 Add the carrots and half of the remaining stock and stir again. Cover and cook for 15 minutes.

5 Add the green leek slices, asparagus and courgettes to the rice, then add a little extra stock. Re-cover and cook for 5–6 minutes, or until the vegetables and rice are just tender.

6 Remove from the heat, stir in the butter and two-thirds of the cheese, and add a little more stock if needed. Top with the mixed leaves, cover with the lid, and warm through for 1–2 minutes or until the leaves are just beginning to wilt.

7 Spoon into shallow bowls, sprinkle with the remaining cheese and serve immediately.

LOVELY LEEKS

Leeks are part of the allium family and contain many antioxidants, minerals and vitamins, including folic acid, niacin, riboflavin and thiamin. They are a good source of vitamin A as well as containing vitamins C, E and K.

PER SERVING: 474 CALS | 17G FAT | 8.1G SAT FAT | 69.4G CARBS | 8.1G SUGARS | 3.8G SALT | 6.4G FIBRE | 14.6G PROTEIN

BEETROOT BURGERS
IN BUNS

*The sweet, earthy flavour of the vegetables in these wholesome
beetroot-and-millet burgers is delicious with the tangy yogurt sauce.*

MAKES: 5 BURGERS
PREP: 30 MINS, PLUS CHILLING   COOK: 35–40 MINS

100 g/3^{1}/$_{2}$ oz millet, rinsed and drained
175 ml/6 fl oz water
1 large raw beetroot (approx 150 g/5^{1}/$_{2}$ oz), grated
30 g/1 oz carrots, grated
175 g/6 oz courgettes, grated
60 g/2^{1}/$_{4}$ oz walnuts, finely chopped
2 tbsp cider vinegar
2 tbsp olive oil, plus extra for frying
1 egg, beaten
2 tbsp cornflour
salt and pepper
5 multi-grain buns, split, to serve
lettuce leaves, to serve

YOGURT SAUCE
225 g/8 oz natural yogurt
2 garlic cloves, finely chopped

1 Put the millet, water and a pinch of salt in a small saucepan. Bring to a simmer over a medium heat, then reduce the heat to low, cover and cook for 20–25 minutes, or until tender. Remove from the heat and leave to stand for 5 minutes, covered.

2 Put the beetroot, carrots, courgettes and walnuts in a large bowl. Add the millet, vinegar, oil, ^{1}/$_{2}$ teaspoon of salt and ^{1}/$_{2}$ teaspoon of pepper and mix well. Add the egg and cornflour, mix again, then cover and chill in the refrigerator for 2 hours.

3 Meanwhile, put the yogurt in a fine sieve over a bowl and leave to drain for at least 30 minutes. Stir in the garlic and season with salt and pepper.

4 Spoon the beetroot mixture into five mounds on a chopping board, then squeeze them into patties using wet hands. Place a ridged griddle pan or large frying pan over a medium heat and coat with olive oil. Add the patties and cook for 10 minutes, or until browned, turning halfway through.

5 Top the base of each bun with a spoonful of the yogurt sauce. Place the burgers on top, then the lettuce, then the bun lid. Serve immediately.

WOW-FACTOR WALNUTS

Eating a handful of walnuts a day could help protect us against heart disease. Scientists have found that they may improve cholesterol levels and blood vessel flexibility.

PER BURGER: 486 CALS | 17.2G FAT | 3G SAT FAT | 70.5G CARBS | 15G SUGARS | 2G SALT | 8.1G FIBRE | 16G PROTEIN

STUFFED RED PEPPERS

A little mince goes a long way in this classic, rustic-style dish that's packed with nutritious pulses.

SERVES: 4   PREP: 20 MINS   COOK: 1 HOUR

4 large red peppers, stalks left on, halved lengthways and deseeded
1 tbsp olive oil
1 red onion, finely chopped
400 g/14 oz lean minced beef
2 garlic cloves, finely chopped
1/4 tsp smoked hot paprika or chilli powder
1 tsp ground cumin
400 g/14 oz canned chickpeas, drained
400 g/14 oz canned green lentils, drained and rinsed
400 g/14 oz canned chopped tomatoes
125 ml/4 fl oz beef stock
salt and pepper
175 g/6 oz 0% fat Greek-style natural yogurt (optional)
15 g/1/2 oz fresh mint, roughly chopped
15 g/1/2 oz fresh flat-leaf parsley, roughly chopped

1   Preheat the oven to 180°C/350°F/Gas Mark 4. Arrange the peppers cut side up in a roasting tin.

2   Heat the oil in a frying pan over a medium heat. Add the red onion, minced beef and garlic and cook, stirring and breaking up the mince, for 5 minutes, or until evenly browned.

3   Stir in the paprika and cumin, then the chickpeas, lentils, tomatoes and stock. Season with salt and pepper, then increase the heat to high and bring to the boil. Remove from the heat.

4   Spoon the mince mixture into the peppers, cover the dish with foil, then bake for 50 minutes, or until the peppers are tender and the mince is cooked.

5   Remove the foil, top each pepper with a spoonful of yogurt, if using, then sprinkle generously with the mint and parsley and serve immediately.

FAB FRAGRANT MINT

Mint is rich in antioxidants and phytonutrients that are thought to be good for the stomach. It has anti-inflammatory properties, so is believed to be beneficial for the skin too. Some health experts also say it relieves headaches and menstrual cramps.

PER SERVING: 466 CALS | 16.2G FAT | 5G SAT FAT | 40.8G CARBS | 11.9G SUGARS | 1.3G SALT | 9.1G FIBRE | 36G PROTEIN

BLACK BEAN AND QUINOA BURRITOS

*This Mexican-American treat is filling enough for a main meal,
but is equally good served cold and packed into a lunch box.*

MAKES: 8 BURRITOS
PREP: 30 MINS   COOK: 20 MINS, PLUS STANDING

60 g/2¼ oz red quinoa, rinsed
150 ml/5 fl oz water
2 tbsp vegetable oil
1 red onion, roughly chopped
1 green chilli, deseeded and finely chopped
1 small red pepper, deseeded and cut into cubes
400 g/14 oz canned black beans, drained and rinsed
juice of 1 lime
15 g/½ oz fresh coriander, roughly chopped
2 tomatoes
8 corn tortillas, warmed
125 g/4½ oz Cheddar cheese, coarsely grated
85 g/3 oz cos lettuce, shredded
salt and pepper

1 Put the quinoa, water and a pinch of salt in a small saucepan. Bring to the boil, then cover and simmer over a very low heat for 15 minutes. Remove from the heat, but leave the pan covered for 5 minutes more to allow the grains to swell. Fluff up with a fork.

2 Heat the oil in a frying pan over a medium heat. Add half the red onion, half the green chilli and half the red pepper and cook until softened. Add the beans, cooked quinoa, half the lime juice and half the coriander and cook for 3–4 minutes. Season with salt and pepper.

3 Halve the tomatoes and scoop out the seeds. Add the seeds to the bean mixture. Finely chop the flesh and transfer it to a bowl. Add the remaining red onion, green chilli, red pepper, lime juice and coriander, season with salt and stir well.

4 Put 5 tablespoons of the bean mixture on top of each tortilla. Sprinkle with the tomato salsa, cheese and lettuce. Fold the end and sides of the tortillas over the filling, roll up and serve.

RAINBOW VEG

Try to broaden the types and colours of the vegetables you eat, the brighter the better for the maximum range of health-protecting antioxidants and phytochemicals in your diet.

PER BURRITO: 270 CALS | 10.4G FAT | 3.9G SAT FAT | 36.7G CARBS | 1.8G SUGARS | 0.7G SALT | 5.2G FIBRE | 9.3G PROTEIN

RAW SHOOTS AND SEEDS SUPER SALAD

Sprouting seeds are bursting with nutrients and low in calories, making this superfood dish super-light as well as super-healthy.

SERVES: 6   PREP: 15 MINS

225 g/8 oz mixed sprouted seeds and beans,
such as alfalfa, mung beans, soy beans, aduki beans,
chickpeas and radish seeds
25 g/1 oz pumpkin seeds
25 g/1 oz sunflower seeds
25 g/1 oz sesame seeds
1 dessert apple, cored and roughly chopped
70 g/2½ oz dried apricots, roughly chopped
finely grated zest and juice of 1 unwaxed lemon
50 g/1¾ oz walnuts, roughly chopped
2 tbsp walnut oil

1 Put the sprouted seeds, pumpkin seeds, sunflower seeds and sesame seeds in a large bowl. Stir in the apple and dried apricots, lemon zest and walnuts.

2 To make the dressing, put the lemon juice and oil in a small bowl and mix together with a fork.

3 Stir the dressing into the salad, then serve immediately.

SPROUTING SEEDS

Sprouting seeds are a quick and easy way of filling up with nutrients. Studies show they contain high levels of the vitamin B group, as well as vitamins A, C and E.

PER SERVING: 228 CALS | 17.8G FAT | 1.9G SAT FAT | 15G CARBS | 8.7G SUGARS | TRACE SALT | 4G FIBRE | 6.7G PROTEIN

DESSERTS AND BAKING

CHOCOLATE, CINNAMON AND VANILLA CUSTARD POTS

Rich, dark and smooth, these easy-to-make desserts look fabulous and will satisfy any chocolate craving.

MAKES: 6 POTS

PREP: 20 MINS   COOK: 50 MINS   CHILL: 5 HOURS

450 ml/15 fl oz semi-skimmed milk
200 g/7 oz 70% plain chocolate, broken into pieces, plus 1 tbsp finely grated plain chocolate to decorate
1 tsp vanilla extract
1/4 tsp ground cinnamon
4 tbsp runny honey
2 eggs, plus 2 egg yolks
90 g/3 1/4 oz 0% fat Greek-style natural yogurt, to decorate

1 Preheat the oven to 150°C/300°F/Gas Mark 2. Pour the milk into a heavy-bottomed saucepan, bring just to the boil, then take off the heat and stir in the chocolate pieces, vanilla extract, cinnamon and 3 tablespoons of honey. Set aside for 5 minutes, or until the chocolate has melted. Stir until the milk is an even dark chocolate colour.

2 Put the eggs and egg yolks in a large jug and beat lightly with a fork. Gradually pour in the warm chocolate milk, beating all the time with a wooden spoon, until smooth. Strain back into the saucepan through a sieve, then press any remaining chocolate through the sieve using the back of the wooden spoon.

3 Put six 175-ml/6-fl oz ovenproof cups or ramekins in a roasting tin. Fill the cups with the chocolate milk, then pour hot water into the roasting tin to reach halfway up the cups. Cover the cups with foil, then bake for 40–45 minutes, or until the custards are just set, with a slight wobble in the centre.

4 Using oven gloves, lift the cups out of the roasting tin and leave to cool, then cover with clingfilm and chill in the refrigerator for 4–5 hours.

5 Place the cups on a serving platter, remove the clingfilm and top each with a spoonful of yogurt, a drizzle of the remaining honey and a little grated chocolate.

PLAIN CHOCOLATE IS GOOD FOR YOU!

Research shows that plain chocolate is packed with antioxidants and may help lower blood pressure, but it must have 65 per cent or ideally more cocoa content. The darker it is, the less fat and sugar it is likely to contain.

PER POT: 343 CALS | 19.5G FAT | 10.6G SAT FAT | 32.3G CARBS | 24.5G SUGARS | 0.2G SALT | 3.8G FIBRE | 10G PROTEIN

CHOCOLATE, FRUIT AND NUT BARK

Hazelnuts and chocolate make this snack a superfood treat that's perfect for wrapping in baking paper and packing into your lunch box.

MAKES: 16 PIECES
PREP: 15 MINS   COOK: 4 MINS   CHILL: 1 HOUR

70 g/2¹/₂ oz dried cherries
55 g/2 oz hazelnuts, roughly chopped
350 g/12 oz 70% plain chocolate, broken into pieces
15 g/¹/₂ oz crispy rice cereal

1 Line a 28 x 23-cm/11 x 9-inch baking tin with baking paper.

2 Put the dried cherries and hazelnuts in a small bowl and mix well.

3 Put the chocolate in a heatproof bowl set over a saucepan of gently simmering water, making sure the bowl doesn't touch the water, and heat until melted. Remove from the heat and stir in the rice cereal.

4 Pour the chocolate mixture into the prepared tin and smooth it into a thin layer using a palette knife. Immediately sprinkle over the dried cherries and hazelnuts, then press them into the chocolate with the palm of your hand. Cover with clingfilm and chill in the refrigerator for 1 hour, or until set.

5 Break into 16 pieces and serve at room temperature.

GO HAZELNUTS!

Hazelnuts are rich in vitamin E, and contain protein and vitamin A. They are loaded with minerals too, especially manganese, selenium and zinc.

PER PIECE: 171 CALS | 11.4G FAT | 5.5G SAT FAT | 15G CARBS | 7.5G SUGARS | TRACE SALT | 3.8G FIBRE | 2.4G PROTEIN

SKINNY BANANA SPLIT SUNDAES

Keep this twist on a traditional sundae in the freezer, then make the chocolate sauce just before serving, for a superfood-packed standby dessert the whole family will love.

SERVES: 2
PREP: 10 MINS   COOK: 6 MINS   FREEZE: 3 HOURS

2 small bananas, peeled and roughly chopped
6 unblanched almonds, roughly chopped

CHOCOLATE SAUCE
30 g/1 oz soft light brown sugar
3 tbsp cocoa powder
6 tbsp semi-skimmed milk
30 g/1 oz 70% plain chocolate, broken into pieces
1/2 tsp vanilla extract

1 Put the bananas in a plastic container and freeze for 2 hours. Transfer to a food processor and process until smooth and creamy. Return to the container, re-cover and freeze for 1 hour, or until firm.

2 To make the chocolate sauce, put the sugar, cocoa powder and milk in a small saucepan and bring to a simmer over a medium heat. Reduce the heat to low and cook, stirring constantly, for 1 minute, or until the sugar and cocoa powder have dissolved.

3 Remove from the heat, then stir in the chocolate until it has melted. Stir in the vanilla extract. Leave to cool slightly.

4 Place a frying pan over a high heat. Add the almonds, cover and dry-fry for 3–4 minutes, or until toasted.

5 Scoop the banana purée into two glasses or bowls, drizzle with the warm chocolate sauce and sprinkle with the almonds.

AMAZING ALMONDS

Almonds are a rich source of calcium, protein, essential fats, B vitamins and vitamin E. They also contain iron, potassium and magnesium, as well as copper, which is needed in red blood cell production and so can help prevent anaemia.

PER SERVING: 311 CALS | 11.3G FAT | 5.1G SAT FAT | 52.9G CARBS | 33.7G SUGARS | TRACE SALT | 7.5G FIBRE | 6.4G PROTEIN

WARM WALNUT AND ORANGE CAKE

A Middle Eastern-inspired cake that is gluten-free and packed with energy-boosting nuts. The whole cooked orange gives it a tangy, high-fibre citrus hit.

MAKES: 10 SLICES PREP: 25 MINS COOK: 2¼ HOURS

3 large whole oranges (approx 250 g/9 oz each)
125 g/4½ oz dried apricots
70 g/2½ oz walnuts, roughly chopped, plus 12 halves to decorate
70 g/2½ oz unblanched almonds, roughly chopped, plus 6 to decorate
70 g/2½ oz Brazil nuts, roughly chopped, plus 12 to decorate
4 eggs
200 g/7 oz golden caster sugar
125 ml/4 fl oz light olive oil, plus extra to grease
85 g/3 oz brown rice flour
2 tsp gluten–free baking powder
250 g/9 oz 0% fat Greek-style natural yogurt, to serve

BRILLIANT BRAZIL NUTS

Brazil nuts are a good source of the mineral selenium, which we need to produce the active thyroid hormone, and which helps boost your immune system. They are also rich in protein and fibre.

1 Put one orange in a small saucepan, just cover with water, then bring to the boil, cover and simmer for 45 minutes. Add the dried apricots, re-cover and cook for 15 minutes, or until the orange is very tender when pierced with a knife. Drain the fruits, reserving the cooking water, and leave to cool.

2 Preheat the oven to 160°C/325°F/Gas Mark 3. Lightly brush a 24-cm/9½-inch round springform cake tin with a little oil. Put the 70 g/2½ oz each of walnuts, almonds and Brazil nuts in a food processor, then process until finely ground. Transfer to a large mixing bowl.

3 Roughly chop the cooked orange, discard any pips, then put it and the apricots in the food processor and process into a coarse purée. Add the eggs, 150 g/5½ oz sugar and all the oil, and process again until smooth.

4 Spoon the brown rice flour and baking powder into the ground nuts and mix well. Tip into the food processor and process briefly, until smooth. Pour the cake mixture into the prepared tin, spread it level with a spatula, and decorate with the walnut halves, whole almonds and whole Brazil nuts.

5 Bake for 1-1¼ hours, or until browned, slightly cracked on top, and a skewer inserted into the centre comes out clean. Check after 40 minutes and loosely cover the top with foil if the nut decoration is browning too quickly.

6 Cut the peel and pith away from the remaining oranges with a small serrated knife. Cut between the membranes to release the segments. Measure 125 ml/4 fl oz of the reserved orange cooking water, making it up with extra water if need be, and pour it into a small saucepan. Add the remaining sugar and cook over a low heat until the sugar has dissolved. Increase the heat to high and boil for 3 minutes, or until you have a syrup. Add the orange segments and leave to cool.

7 Loosen the edge of the cake with a round-bladed knife and turn out onto a wire rack. Leave to cool slightly, then cut into wedges and serve warm, with the oranges in syrup and spoonfuls of the Greek yogurt.

PER SLICE: 517 CALS | 33.7G FAT | 5.3G SAT FAT | 47.4G CARBS | 34.6G SUGARS | 0.8G SALT | 5.2G FIBRE | 11.9G PROTEIN

SUMMER BERRY SPONGE CAKES

These light sponge cakes are made without butter and filled with fat-free Greek yogurt for a sweet treat that doesn't look or taste low calorie.

MAKES: 6 CAKES   PREP: 25 MINS   COOK: 15 MINS

oil, to grease
3 eggs
85 g/3 oz golden caster sugar
1/2 tsp vanilla extract
85 g/3 oz brown rice flour
250 g/9 oz 0% fat Greek-style natural yogurt
400 g/14 oz mixed raspberries, blueberries, and hulled and sliced strawberries
1 tbsp icing sugar, sifted

1 Preheat the oven to 180°C/350°F/Gas Mark 4. Brush six 175-ml/6-fl oz ring mould tins with a little oil and put them on a baking sheet.

2 Put the eggs, caster sugar and vanilla extract in a large bowl and beat with an electric hand-held whisk for 5 minutes, or until the mixture is thick and leaves a trail when the whisk is lifted.

3 Sift the flour over the egg mixture, then gently fold it in with a large metal spoon. Spoon the mixture into the tins and ease it into an even layer, being careful not to knock out any air.

4 Bake for 12–15 minutes, or until the cakes are risen and golden brown and beginning to shrink away from the edges.

5 Leave to cool in the tins for 5 minutes. Loosen the edges of the cakes with a round-bladed knife and turn them out onto a wire rack. Leave to cool completely.

6 Put the cakes on serving plates, spoon the yogurt into the centre, then pile the fruits on top. Dust with sifted icing sugar and serve.

RASPBERRY GOODNESS

Raspberries are bursting with vitamin C and contain powerful antioxidants that are thought to help boost the immune system and protect us from cancers. They are also rich in B-complex vitamins and vitamin K.

PER CAKE: 219 CALS | 4.5G FAT | 1G SAT FAT | 36.3G CARBS | 22.6G SUGARS | 0.1G SALT | 2.8G FIBRE | 9.3G PROTEIN

CREAMY COCONUT AND MANGO QUINOA

Forget white rice, this healthy take on rice pudding is made with nutrient-dense quinoa.

SERVES: 4

PREP: 15 MINS, PLUS STANDING   COOK: 20 MINS

300 ml/10 fl oz canned coconut milk
115 g/4 oz quinoa, rinsed
350 g/12 oz mango flesh, roughly chopped
75 g/2³⁄4 oz golden caster sugar
juice of 1 large lime
4-cm/1¹⁄2-inch piece fresh ginger, peeled and cut into chunks
100 g/3¹⁄2 oz blueberries
4 tbsp toasted dried coconut shavings

1 Put the coconut milk and quinoa in a small saucepan and bring to the boil over a medium heat. Reduce the heat to low, cover and simmer for 10–15 minutes, or until most of the liquid has evaporated. Remove from the heat and set aside for 7 minutes more to allow the grains to swell. Fluff up with a fork, tip into a bowl and leave to cool.

2 Meanwhile, put the mango, sugar and lime juice in a food processor. Squeeze the ginger through a garlic press and add the juice to the food processor. Process for 30 seconds, or until you have a smooth purée.

3 Mix the mango purée into the cooled quinoa, then cover and leave to stand for 30 minutes.

4 Spoon the mixture into four bowls and sprinkle with the blueberries and coconut shavings. Serve immediately.

BRILLIANT BLUEBERRIES

Blueberries have a high concentration of antioxidants, which are thought to help prevent heart disease and even cancer. They are rich in manganese, fibre, which helps keep your cholesterol low, and vitamin C for immunity.

PER SERVING: 408 CALS | 16.7G FAT | 13.2G SAT FAT | 60.8G CARBS | 37.2G SUGARS | TRACE SALT | 5G FIBRE | 6.5G PROTEIN

GRILLED STONE FRUIT POTS

When you need a glamorous dessert but you're in a rush, these low-fat pots bursting with fresh fruit are just the thing!

SERVES: 6   PREP: 10 MINS   COOK: 5 MINS

375 g/13 oz low-fat ricotta cheese
2 tsp finely grated orange zest
3 peaches, stoned and quartered
3 nectarines, stoned and quartered
3 plums or apricots, stoned and quartered
2 tbsp honey, ideally orange-blossom
2 tbsp flaked almonds

1 Preheat the grill to medium-high. Line the grill rack with foil.

2 Put the ricotta and orange zest in a bowl and stir well.

3 Lay all the fruit in a single layer on the foil-lined grill rack. Grill, turning halfway, for 5 minutes, or until softened and beginning to caramelize.

4 Spoon the ricotta into six glasses. Top each with some grilled fruit, drizzle with the honey and sprinkle with the flaked almonds. Serve immediately.

REACH FOR APRICOTS

Apricots are rich in beta-carotene, which is important for vision, and vitamin C. They are also a good source of fibre and minerals such as potassium and manganese.

PER SERVING: 202 CALS | 7.1G FAT | 3.2G SAT FAT | 28.1G CARBS | 21.2G SUGARS | 0.2G SALT | 3.2G FIBRE | 9.5G PROTEIN

CRANBERRY AND RASPBERRY JELLY

Beloved of children's parties, jelly is popular with all ages — and it's virtually fat free! This cranberry jelly has a delicious grown-up flavour and beautiful colour.

**SERVES: 6 PREP: 15 MINS
COOK: 15 MINS CHILL AND FREEZE: 7¹/₄ HOURS**

350 g/12 oz frozen cranberries
85 g/3 oz golden caster sugar
600 ml/1 pint water, plus extra for the gelatine
15 g/¹/₂ oz leaf gelatine
175 g/6 oz frozen raspberries, plus a few extra to serve

1 Put the frozen cranberries, sugar and 225 ml/8 fl oz water in a saucepan, cover and cook over a medium heat for 10–15 minutes, or until soft. Leave to cool.

2 Meanwhile, put the gelatine sheets in a shallow dish, cover with cold water and leave to soften for 5 minutes.

3 Pour the cranberries and their cooking liquid into a food processor and process to a purée. Push the purée through a sieve back into the saucepan, then stir in the remaining water and warm over a low heat.

4 Drain the gelatine sheets, add to the warm cranberry mixture and stir until the gelatine is dissolved. Leave to cool.

5 Arrange a ring of frozen raspberries in the base of a 1.2-litre/2-pint jelly mould, then spoon a little of the cranberry mixture over the top. Freeze for 15–20 minutes, or until set.

6 Pour half the remaining cranberry mixture into the mould, sprinkle with half the remaining raspberries, then chill in the refrigerator for 1 hour, or until just set. Pour the remaining cranberry mixture over the raspberries and sprinkle over the remaining raspberries. Chill in the refrigerator for 4–6 hours, or until set firm.

7 Dip the mould into a bowl of hot water, count to ten, then lift it out. Invert the mould onto a plate, then, holding the mould and the plate tightly, jerk to release the jelly. Remove the mould and serve.

CRANBERRY PROTECTION

These bright-red, tart-tasting berries are rich in vitamins C and A and potassium. Their phytochemicals may help prevent and aid recovery from cystitis and other urinary tract infections.

PER SERVING: 106 CALS | 0.3G FAT | TRACE SAT FAT | 25.3G CARBS | 18G SUGARS | TRACE SALT | 4.8G FIBRE | 2.4G PROTEIN

STRAWBERRIES WITH BALSAMIC VINEGAR

Proving simplicity really can be best, this summer dessert combines sweetness, spice and acidity in the most delicious way! Be sure to use only the best strawberries.

SERVES: 4   PREP: 5 MINS   STAND: 3 HOURS

2 tbsp golden caster sugar
1 tbsp balsamic vinegar
400 g/14 oz strawberries, hulled and halved
pepper

1 Put the sugar and vinegar in a non-metallic bowl and stir. Add the strawberries and stir well. Leave to stand for at least 1 hour, but for no more than 3 hours.

2 Stir again, then add extra sugar or vinegar if desired.

3 Grind some pepper over the top of the strawberries and serve immediately.

SENSATIONAL STRAWBERRIES

Strawberries contain a lot of vitamin C and are relatively high in fibre. They are also an excellent source of the mineral manganese, which is good for bone health.

PER SERVING: 64 CALS | 0.3G FAT | TRACE SAT FAT | 15.7G CARBS | 12.5G SUGARS | TRACE SALT | 2.2G FIBRE | 0.7G PROTEIN

GREEN TEA FRUIT SALAD

The delicate and refreshing taste of green tea works well mixed with chopped fresh mint and a hint of honey in a syrup for a fruit salad.

SERVES: 4   PREP: 15 MINS   CHILL: 1 HOUR

2 tsp green tea
225 ml/8 fl oz boiling water
1 tbsp runny honey
½ small watermelon, deseeded, peeled and cut into cubes
1 large mango, stoned, peeled and cut into cubes
1 papaya, deseeded, peeled and cut into cubes
2 pears, peeled, cored and cut into cubes
2 kiwi fruit, peeled and cut into cubes
2 tbsp roughly chopped fresh mint
seeds of ½ pomegranate
2 tbsp roughly chopped pistachio nuts

1 Put the tea in a jug or teapot, pour over the boiling water and leave to brew for 3–4 minutes. Strain into a small bowl, stir in the honey and leave to cool.

2 Put the watermelon, mango and papaya in a large serving bowl, then add the pears, kiwi fruit and mint. Pour over the cooled green tea and stir gently.

3 Cover the fruit salad with clingfilm and chill in the refrigerator for 1 hour. Stir gently to mix the tea through the fruit.

4 Spoon the fruit salad into four bowls and serve sprinkled with the pomegranate seeds and pistachio nuts.

GO FOR GREEN TEA

Green tea is used in traditional Chinese medicine. It contains antioxidants, and is thought to have antibacterial and antiviral properties.

PER SERVING: 313 CALS | 4.8G FAT | 0.6G SAT FAT | 70.8G CARBS | 54G SUGARS | TRACE SALT | 10G FIBRE | 5.2G PROTEIN

RASPBERRY AND WATERMELON SORBET

Wonderfully refreshing on a hot day, or soothing after a spicy main course,
this healthy and easy-to-make dessert is great to have tucked away in the freezer.

SERVES: 4   PREP: 20 MINS
COOK: 4 MINS   FREEZE: 8 HOURS

115 g/4 oz golden caster sugar
150 ml/5 fl oz cold water
finely grated zest and juice of 1 lime
225 g/8 oz raspberries
1 small watermelon, deseeded, peeled and
cut into chunks
1 egg white

1 Put the sugar, water and lime zest in a small saucepan and cook over a low heat, stirring, until the sugar has dissolved. Increase to high until the mixture comes to a boil, then reduce the heat to medium and simmer for 3–4 minutes. Leave to cool completely.

2 Put the raspberries and watermelon in a food processor in batches and process to a purée, then press through a sieve into a bowl to remove any remaining seeds.

3 Tip the purée into a loaf tin, pour in the lime syrup through a sieve, then stir in the lime juice. Freeze for 3–4 hours, or until the sorbet is beginning to freeze around the edges and the centre is still mushy.

4 Transfer the sorbet to a food processor and process to break up the ice crystals. Put the egg white in a small bowl and lightly whisk with a fork until frothy, then mix it into the sorbet.

5 Pour the sorbet into a plastic or metal container, cover and freeze for 3–4 hours, or until firm. Allow to soften at room temperature for 10–15 minutes before serving. Eat within a week of freezing.

WONDERFUL WATERMELON

Watermelon contains 90 per cent water, making it good for rehydrating the body. Unlike alcohol or caffeine, it is gentle on the kidneys. Choose the deepest red-fleshed melon you can find for greater amounts of the carotenoid pigment lycopene, which is important for its antioxidant properties and cardiovascular health.

PER SERVING: 210 CALS | 0.7G FAT | TRACE SAT FAT | 52.4G CARBS | 44G SUGARS | TRACE SALT | 4.9G FIBRE | 2.9G PROTEIN

FRUIT COCKTAIL ICE LOLLIES

This is a wonderful way to capture the essence of summer, with the flavours and vibrant colours of ripe, juicy peaches, strawberries and kiwis.

MAKES: 8 ICE LOLLIES
PREP: 15 MINS   COOK: 12 MINS   FREEZE: 8 HOURS

30 g/1 oz golden caster sugar
4^1/$_2$ tbsp water
200 g/7 oz strawberries, hulled
225 g/8 oz peaches, peeled, stoned and roughly chopped (or 200 g/7 oz canned peaches)
4 large kiwi fruit, peeled and roughly chopped

1 Put the sugar and water in a small saucepan and cook over a low heat, stirring, for 5–6 minutes, or until all the sugar has dissolved. Increase the heat to high until the mixture comes to a boil, then reduce the heat to medium and simmer for 3–4 minutes. Leave to cool completely.

2 Put the strawberries in a blender and process until puréed. Stir in a third of the sugar syrup. Pour the mixture into 8 x 100-ml/3^1/$_2$-fl oz ice lolly moulds. Freeze for 2 hours, or until firm.

3 When the strawberry mixture is frozen, put the peaches in the blender and process until puréed. Stir in half of the remaining sugar syrup. Pour this over the frozen strawberry mixture. Insert the ice lolly sticks and freeze for 2 hours, or until firm.

4 When the peach mixture is frozen, put the kiwi fruit in the blender and process until puréed. Stir in the remaining sugar syrup. Pour this over the frozen peach mixture and freeze for 2 hours, or until firm.

5 To unmould the ice lollies, dip the frozen moulds into warm water for a few seconds and gently release the lollies while holding the sticks.

COOL KIWI

Kiwi fruit is a good source of fibre and vitamins A, C and K. It is also rich in potassium and folate.

PER ICE LOLLY: 57 CALS | 0.3G FAT | TRACE SAT FAT | 14G CARBS | 11.1G SUGARS | TRACE SALT | 2G FIBRE | 0.8G PROTEIN

INDEX